# Labour markets in transition

## Balancing flexibility &security in Central and Eastern Europe

# Labour markets in transition

## Balancing flexibility & security in Central and Eastern Europe

*Sandrine Cazes*
*Alena Nesporova*

International Labour Office ● Geneva

Cazes, S.; Nesporova, A.
*Labour markets in transition: Balancing flexibility and security in Central and Eastern Europe*
Geneva, International Labour Office, 2003

Labour flexibility, employment, employment security, labour policy, CIS country, Eastern Europe. 13.01.2

ISBN 92-2-113723-6

Cover design: © Aimery Chaigne 2003

*ILO Cataloguing in Publication Data*

Typeset by Magheross Graphics, France & Ireland *www.magheross.com*
Printed in

# FOREWORD

The research for this book has been guided by the International Labour Organization (ILO) Employment Sector's main activity, the Global Employment Agenda for the pursuit of Decent Work for All, approved by the ILO Governing Body in March 2003. One key element of the Global Employment Agenda is successful management of labour market changes, provoked by global competition and technological progress, with the help of social and labour market policies: policies improving the capacity, mobility and flexibility of workers, but requiring adequate employment and income security in exchange. While the Agenda provides a framework for this type of research and discussion of its policy implications, the latter contribute to its further elaboration in the regional and national context.

More specifically, this monograph is the outcome of an ongoing ILO technical project on flexicurity, being carried out in developed, transition and developing countries. It is aimed at analysing the relationship between flexibility, stability, security, labour market performance and productivity with the overarching long-term goal of achieving full, productive and freely chosen employment at the global, regional, national and local levels. The book fills a gap in the existing literature on this important topic for the special case of transition countries of Central and Eastern Europe. The results of cross-country comparisons within the group of selected transition countries, as well as with the countries of the European Union and the Organisation for Economic Co-operation and Development, and the related suggested labour market policy conclusions could be very interesting for policy-makers both from governments and the social partners, giving them ideas about how to better manage labour market changes from an economic and social point of view.

The labour markets of the former command economies of Central and Eastern Europe and Central Asia have gone through profound transformation since the start of their political, economic and social reforms. While in the past, full employment had been guaranteed by the State and the countries had even experienced labour shortages, after 1989 they were suddenly confronted with accelerating unemployment that remained fairly high and persistent. Neither the labour legislation nor the labour market institutions were able to handle this new situation properly. Enterprises requested more freedom to reduce massive labour hoarding and adjust their workforce to production and economic changes, while large numbers of laid-off workers needed assistance in finding new jobs, improving their skills and managing an abrupt loss of income. National authorities responded by amending labour legislation and establishing national employment services aimed at providing job search assistance for the unemployed. They also introduced labour market policies for improving jobseekers' employability and for interventions on both the demand and supply sides of the labour market.

The exposure of enterprises from emerging economies to competition in global markets has been forcing them to rationalize production costs, including labour, and to react rapidly to market changes. Besides downsizing, they have also started offering workers time-limited labour contracts, contracts regulated by the Civil Code or informal employment with no contract at all, and making partial payments of wages "under the table" to evade taxation. However, confronted with this tendency towards flexible forms of employment and higher informal employment, and the consequent significant weakening of workers' employment and social protection, governments have had to further amend existing labour legislation and also to think about more effective assistance to workers. Social dialogue has been playing an increasingly important role in this process, at both the national and enterprise level. The issue is now to find a new balance between appropriate adjustment flexibility for enterprises, which would remove impediments to productivity improvements, and reasonable employment and income security for workers, contributing towards the reduction of unemployment and poverty.

While economically developed countries have recognized and addressed the need to analyse the type of labour market regulations necessary to ensure this "flexicurity", for the transition countries it is currently a very important issue. Both employers and workers in transition countries are of the opinion that their justified requirements are not being properly tackled by labour law amendments or by labour market and social policies, and that they are being disadvantaged vis-à-vis their competitors or other groups of the population. Developed countries vary considerably in the possible combinations of different types of employment protection and labour market policy (such as potential trade-offs or complementarities), but the prevailing trend is towards facilitating higher adjustment flexibility for enterprises while compensating it with broader employment security for workers outside the enterprise. As workers now face less protection against dismissals, for them to accept this eventuality they need to feel secure in terms of getting more assistance from labour market institutions in re-employment, reasonable income support and better access to labour market programmes.

This book aims to contribute to this debate on the degree of flexibility and security needed for the transition countries, and its implications for the new direction of labour market and social policies. Analytical findings show that on average transition countries are not falling behind in relaxing their labour market regulations relative to those of economically developed countries, but that the law enforcement and labour market institutions and policies in the transition countries are still rather weak and support high employment and job insecurity. Much more needs to be done in this respect and the book suggests some promising policy improvements to remedy this important shortcoming, which has negative social and economic consequences.

*Göran Hultin*
*Executive Director*
*Employment Sector, ILO*

# CONTENTS

**List of tables**

## List of figures

## List of boxes

# ACKNOWLEDGEMENTS

Thanks go to the following researchers who provided statistical information and prepared country studies on flexibility and security: Iskra Beleva and Vasyl Tzanov from Bulgaria, Jiří Večerník from the Czech Republic, Reelika Arro, Raul Eamets, Janno Järva, Epp Kallaste and Kaia Philips from Estonia, Eugeniusz Kwiatkowski, Mieczysław Socha and Urszula Sztanderska from Poland, and Tatyana Tchetvernina, Alexandra Moscovskaya, Irina Soboleva and Natalya Stepantchikova from the Russian Federation, and Sylvie Rauffet for providing statistical assistance. The authors also benefited from valuable comments given by the three reviewers, as well as from discussions with a number of ILO colleagues on earlier drafts of individual chapters that appeared as ILO working papers or articles.

Further, the authors would like to express their sincere gratitude to Petra Ulshoefer, Director of the Sub-Regional Office in Budapest, for all her support in the period of finalization of the manuscript and her excellent ideas on how to promote the findings and policy conclusions in the ILO's continuing cooperation with the constituents in Central and Eastern Europe.

Finally, thanks are due to Charlotte Beauchamp for her careful editing of the manuscript and to Aimery Chaigne for the excellent design of the cover pages.

# INTRODUCTION: THE CASE FOR LABOUR MARKET INSTITUTIONS IN TRANSITION COUNTRIES

**1**

## 1.1 LABOUR MARKET FLEXIBILITY

One of the most consistently controversial labour market issues is whether or not the poor employment performance of the European countries (relative to the United States) is the consequence of the rigidities of their labour markets. Some economists clearly attribute the high levels of unemployment that persist in Europe to the inflexible labour markets in these countries, while others reject this view. On the one hand, the "low road" of higher labour market flexibility is proposed as a remedy for the "sclerosis" of the European labour markets: neo-liberal economists advocate more flexible labour markets by weakening, for example, labour market regulations,[1] reflecting the Organisation for Economic Co-operation and Development (OECD) *Jobs Study* view (OECD, 1994a). On the other hand, many other studies (including the OECD 1999 *Employment Outlook*) found no influence of employment protection legislation[2] on the level of unemployment (although some negative impact was revealed on the structure of unemployment). Indeed, the popular perception of the adverse role of employment protection on employment and unemployment is challenged by several labour market experts. Pissarides, for example, notes that "workers usually seek employment protection and employers do not appear to oppose it as vigorously as some economists do" (Pissarides, 2001, p. 133). There is no convincing evidence that firms themselves would opt for a very high degree of flexibility and high labour turnover. They may prefer stable employment relationships and appreciate experience, as transaction costs such as screening and training would be lower and efficiency wages are counted over

---

[1] Labour market regulations include here labour market institutions (trade unions, unemployment insurance systems, public employment services, and so on), legislation (employment protection legislation, law on minimum wages, and so on) and labour market policies.

[2] Employment protection legislation refers to regulatory provisions that relate to hiring and firing practices, particularly those governing unfair dismissals, termination of employment for economic reasons, severance payments, minimum notice periods, administrative authorization for dismissals, and prior consultations with trade union and/or labour administration representatives.

the longer term (see the human capital school, Becker, 1964, and the "new institutionalists", such as Williamson, 1985).

The complexity of the concept of "labour market flexibility" may also feed its ideological dimension: broadly speaking, adjustment is identified with flexibility, and rigidity is commonly opposed to it. At the macro level, flexibility refers to the speed of adjustment to external shocks or changing labour market conditions. Therefore, labour market flexibility means the degree to which employment and/or working time (labour input adjustment) or wages (labour costs adjustment) adjust to economic changes. There are indeed different definitions of labour market flexibility. There is external versus internal flexibility, the former referring to job changes involving new employment with a different employer and relating to labour turnover and geographic mobility, and the latter referring to job changes within the same enterprise. There is also numerical versus functional flexibility, the former relating to changes in the number of workers, and the latter meaning occupational changes and mobility within the enterprise. This book focuses on external numerical flexibility, through both a macro- and microeconomic perspective, with a particular emphasis on labour market regulations and institutions. The reason for this choice is, first, because we believe these are among the most relevant aspects of labour market flexibility; and, second, because of the current unavailability of data on functional flexibility.

## 1.2    CHANGING LABOUR MARKETS

Labour markets of the former command economies of Central and Eastern Europe and Central Asia have gone through profound transformation since the start of political, economic and social reforms. Until 1990, enterprises had been largely protected against the impacts of the world markets through centrally organized production and distribution, and the dominance of producers in the home market. In addition, labour markets were strongly regulated so that workers enjoyed very high employment security and job stability. The opening up of the national economies of transition countries to global competition has forced domestic enterprises to adjust their inputs (including labour), production technology and outputs to market demand.

After 12 years of transition, persistent unemployment remains a major problem throughout the region. While in some countries this problem was to some extent explained by slow economic recovery, there is enough evidence that even in those countries where economic growth has been relatively high over a longer period, employment, after a large initial decline, has continued to stagnate (Nesporova, 1999). In the early nineties, it was broadly accepted by policy-makers and the population at large that full employment and the relatively generous previous social protection systems could no longer be maintained. Within the structural adjustment package, introducing employment flexibility and lowering social protection were in most cases offered as the sole means with which to transform labour markets in new market conditions. Amended national labour legislation, newly established public employment services and labour market policies have facilitated these changes by reducing high employment protection in existing jobs inherited from the previous regime. In its place is a more broadly conceived employment security to be achieved through the provision of employment services, income support and active labour market programmes. However, the weaknesses in the labour market institutions and in collective bargaining, combined with poor law enforcement, have contributed to a high level of labour market flexibility and a popular perception of job insecurity felt by workers.

The challenge for policy-makers in transition countries is now to develop innovative policies which can better manage labour market changes from an economic and social point of view. Auer and Cazes (2003) give examples of Western industrialized countries that have organized their systems of employment and social protection in a way that allows flexibility for firms while ensuring income (and broader social) protection to workers at the societal level. These examples strongly suggest that it is not one component of the institutional setting alone which determines the question of flexibility and security, but the interactions of the main national labour market institutions, such as unemployment benefit schemes, wage-setting institutions and early retirement schemes.

## 1.3 TRADE-OFFS AND COMPLEMENTARITIES

Various interactions of the different institutional settings may influence the labour market behaviour of individuals and firms. These links may be characterized as trade-offs and/or complementarities. A trade-off exists if one item is "traded" against another. For example, employment protection stringency could be "traded" against more generous unemployment benefits. Complementarities exist if one has protection on both counts: high employment protection legislation and high social protection (Esping-Andersen's "welfare capitalism", very often found in continental European welfare states; Esping-Andersen, 1990). While, in the trade-off case, one might compensate the weak protection on the company level by stronger social protection, this is not the case with complementarity. The notion of complementarity can be understood here as one institutional scheme being reinforced by another (for example, employment protection reinforced by labour market policy), but also in the sense that one item cannot exist without the other. Some of these points were also discussed in Bertola et al. (2000), who found several links between employment protection legislation and other labour market institutions.

These interrelations between the different institutional provisions have of course a national (employment system) dimension. The Danish system, for example, combines high numerical flexibility of its labour market with a high degree of social, income and employability security. The Japanese employment system, by contrast, combines low numerical flexibility with high functional flexibility. With a labour market characterized by "lifetime jobs", Japan has not followed the European practice of mass early retirements and social plans: companies and the public sector are bound (socially if not always legally) to deliver employment security and policies (for example, unemployment insurance) that support employment maintenance, rather than lay-offs.

Different combinations exist,[3] characterizing a national institutional setting. However, the picture becomes more complex, and trade-offs and complementarities seem to operate differently, once sub-elements of the employment system are analysed. Labour market regulations are introduced with the objectives of improving workers' welfare through protection against unjust lay-offs, and through unemployment benefits or/and social security programmes. Employment security, for example, continues to rank high in job desirability ratings and in workforce evaluations of job satisfaction.[4] But because they also imply costs for the parties involved, high employment termination costs may discourage employers from recruiting new workers while higher benefits may reduce employment by catching unemployed people in a benefit trap and not pushing them to take up new jobs. Employment legislation may also protect some workers at the expense of others such as young people, women or the long-term unemployed. This means that a distinction needs to be made between insiders and outsiders;[5] between internal employment security (delivered by private or public employers) and broad employment security (extending beyond internal labour markets and taking account of labour market policy and social security provisions); between the legal and regulatory framework and its implementation/enforcement (see Bertola et al., 2000); and between laws and their enforcement taken together, and real measurable flows on the labour market.

## 1.4 IMPLICATIONS FOR EMPLOYMENT ANALYSIS AND POLICY ADVICE

Choices have to be made on the basis of various combinations (trade-offs and/or complementarities) of the different components of the employment and social protection systems, which need to be identified to allow and ensure a balance between labour market flexibility and employment security. Policy-makers in transition countries have therefore wider choices at their disposal within a given macroeconomic, institutional and political context. The social partners (employers and workers) in these countries are also recognizing that without competitive enterprises which are able to adjust their workforce in numbers, structure and quality to market conditions, employment performance will be poor. At the same time, workers need reasonable employment and income security to be motivated to accept

---

[3] The French and the American systems are also analysed in detail in Auer and Cazes (2003).

[4] Among the main determinants of job satisfaction are high earnings, long job tenure – i.e. the length of time a worker has been continuously employed by the same employer – and relative job security due to a permanent contract; in contrast, low earnings and a precarious job status due to a temporary contract negatively impact on the quality of a job, as measured by self-reported levels of job satisfaction (European Commission, 2001, p. 67).

[5] While the concept of insiders and outsiders seen from the enterprise perspective does not necessarily refer to the distinction between employed and unemployed (as it might include those with a weak attachment to the labour market who often change insider with outsider status), it is safe to admit that much of the insider/outsider theory is in fact based on the distinction between the employed and the unemployed (Lindbeck and Snower, 2001).

higher mobility and flexibility, to increase their productivity and to lower their opposition to change.

Such compromises have been established in the Danish system, which is an illustration of the successful introduction of "flexicurity". The "flexicurity" approach is in line with the ILO's Decent Work Agenda[6] and the European Union (EU) employment policy reflected in the conclusions of the EU Summits in Lisbon and Barcelona. It has strong implications for the ILO's Global Employment Agenda (ILO, 2002), since it questions both the access to employment and the quality of this employment. One key element of the Global Employment Agenda is successful management of labour market changes with the help of social and labour market policies, which will improve the capacity, mobility and flexibility of workers but provide them with adequate employment and income security in exchange. The analysis conducted in this book contributes to this objective for transition countries, where the topic is in the initial stages of serious discussions, in suggesting desirable forms of labour market regulations and especially labour market policies that should accompany changing labour markets.

For policy advice, this approach is important as it shows that trade-offs between employment flexibility and social protection can exist. For the social partners this means an enlarged bargaining area, as the country cannot cut back on employment protection without adding to social protection, or vice versa, if the "flexicurity" system is to be maintained. Core labour market stability is a necessary condition for higher levels of development. Consequently, the institutions supporting this form of efficient stability, for example, social dialogue and labour market policies, need to be built up or reinforced. Efficient institutions are those that find a reasonable balance, acceptable to both sides, between the security needs of workers and the adjustment needs of firms.

This book consists of seven chapters. After this introductory chapter, Chapter 2 presents an overview and analysis of labour market developments – labour market participation, employment, unemployment, underemployment and inactivity – in Central and Eastern Europe and Central Asia over the 1990s. Chapter 3 studies changes in the sectoral structure of employment as well as changes in major characteristics of employment, such as employment status, type of labour contract, formal/informal employment and others, in a cross-country analysis. Chapter 4 focuses on labour market dynamics in selected transition countries in the 1990s. It assesses the levels of employment stability and flexibility, and analyses and explains their changes in connection with the business cycle. The following two chapters investigate the causality between the character of labour market institutions and labour market outcomes. In Chapter 5, the strictness of employment protection legislation is studied, analysing its effect on the level and structure of employment

---

[6] The ILO's Decent Work Agenda aims to promote opportunities for women and men to obtain decent and productive work, in conditions of freedom, equity, security and human dignity. This overarching objective embraces four strategic objectives, namely promoting rights at work; the generation of employment and incomes; extending social protection and social security; and strengthening social dialogue (ILO, 1999).

and unemployment for both selected transition countries and Western industrialized countries. Chapter 6 first examines developments in labour market institutions, labour market policies, collective bargaining and labour taxation in ten transition countries and compares them with selected OECD countries. Then it studies the impacts of labour market institutions, social dialogue and labour taxation on several aggregate labour market indicators by conducting an econometric analysis. Chapter 7 draws general conclusions from our findings and makes recommendations for the future orientation of labour market policy in the transition countries.

Finally, it should be noted that apart from a brief study of the extent and characteristics of employment in the informal economy in transition countries provided in Chapter 2, the main analysis in this book concentrates solely on formal employment because of the availability of statistical data. At the same time we admit that the sharp increase in the informal economy experienced in the 1990s has to be seen as an important part of the process of labour market flexibilization.

# LABOUR MARKET DEVELOPMENTS IN THE 1990s: AN OVERVIEW OF THE TRANSITION COUNTRIES

# 2

This chapter analyses labour market trends experienced by the transition countries of Central and Eastern Europe and Central Asia (CEECA)[1] and tries to identify factors behind the region's disappointingly poor employment performance and persistently high unemployment. It begins with an overview of labour market developments in these countries, identifying some marked differences between the Central and South-Eastern European (CSEE)[2] transition countries (including the Baltic States)[3] and those countries grouped in the Commonwealth of Independent States (CIS).[4] It argues that the reasons for these differences lie in the diversity of existing economic conditions in the countries at the outset of transition and the variety of their economic reforms, institutional arrangements and policies. The chapter explores the effects of different macroeconomic policies adopted and the slow progress of institutional reforms. Demographic factors, as well as variations in education, and in labour market and social policies, are evaluated from the perspective of their impact on labour supply and its match with demand. The role of labour market policy, income policy and collective bargaining is also examined.

---

[1] The CEECA countries are Albania, Armenia, Azerbaijan, Belarus, Bosnia and Herzegovina, Bulgaria, Croatia, Czech Republic, Estonia, Georgia, Hungary, Kazakhstan, Kyrgyzstan, Latvia, Lithuania, Poland, Republic of Moldova, Romania, Russian Federation, Slovakia, Slovenia, Tajikistan, The former Yugoslav Republic of Macedonia, Turkmenistan, Ukraine, Uzbekistan, Yugoslavia.

[2] The CSEE countries are Albania, Bosnia and Herzegovina, Bulgaria, Croatia, Czech Republic, Estonia, Hungary, Latvia, Lithuania, Poland, Romania, Slovakia, Slovenia, The former Yugoslav Republic of Macedonia, Yugoslavia.

[3] The Baltic States are Estonia, Latvia and Lithuania.

[4] The CIS is made up of Armenia, Azerbaijan, Belarus, Georgia, Kazakhstan, Kyrgyzstan, Republic of Moldova, Russian Federation, Tajikistan, Turkmenistan, Ukraine, Uzbekistan.

## 2.1 LABOUR MARKET TRENDS: COMMON FEATURES AND DIFFERENCES ACROSS TRANSITION COUNTRIES

### 2.1.1 Decline in employment

The labour market situation of the former centrally planned economies of CEECA at the onset of transition was characterized by full employment, no open unemployment (with the exception of the former Yugoslavia) and an excess of labour demand over supply. However, full employment was achieved at the cost of low wages, with a demotivating effect on workers. Widespread overstaffing (labour hoarding) occurred in many sectors and serious distortions in the allocation of labour in industry contributed to low levels of labour productivity. The economic reforms launched in the wake of political changes were directed at eliminating these negative characteristics, while social reforms were aimed at making these changes socially acceptable and fiscally affordable.

Almost overnight, national economies were opened to world markets through the introduction of economic measures that allowed rapid price liberalization, combined with strict macroeconomic stabilization policies. The result was a sharp decline in the economic performance of these countries: a decline much steeper than originally expected. Demand for labour collapsed immediately and, after a short lull, employment also started to fall. Even at this early stage, a significant difference in employment trends had emerged between the transition countries of the CSEE and those of the CIS, with the three Baltic States moving gradually from the second to the first group. In the CSEE region, the fall in employment was already dramatic in the nascent years of economic transition, mostly due to the sharp slump in production (see table 2.1).

To facilitate cross-country comparisons in this chapter, the transition decade has been roughly divided into two phases: the 1990–94 period of profound, initial changes driven by major economic and social reforms, in combination with macroeconomic austerity measures and intense external shocks; and the 1995–2000 period of relative economic stabilization. A comparison of production and employment trends reveals that some countries, such as the Czech Republic, Romania, Slovakia and Slovenia, were able to keep employment losses well below those of production, at the cost of further losses in labour productivity. Others, such as Bulgaria, Hungary and Poland, achieved labour productivity increases by sharper cuts in employment.

However, again in contrast with initial assumptions, employment performance did not improve significantly in a number of countries that began this initial period with relatively high economic growth. Indeed, in the Czech Republic, Hungary and Poland, for example, employment continued to decline for several years and then stabilized with only a negligible recovery. In those countries directly or indirectly affected by the Balkan conflict, or unable to sustain economic growth due to serious

Table 2.1   Gross domestic product (GDP) and employment in transition
economies: Average annual growth rates, selected years (percentages)

| Country | GDP | | Employment | |
|---|---|---|---|---|
| | 1990–94 | 1994–2000 | 1990–94 | 1994–2000 |
| Albania | −5.6 | 6.2 | −5.0 | −1.4 |
| Armenia | −16.2 | 5.4 | −2.2 | −2.5 |
| Azerbaijan | −17.0 | 3.7 | −0.5 | 0.3 |
| Belarus | −7.8 | 3.3 | −2.3 | −0.9 |
| Bulgaria | −3.9 | −0.6 | −5.7 | −1.6 |
| Croatia | −9.3 | 4.2 | −6.3 | 0.5 |
| Czech Republic | −2.6 | 1.8 | −2.3 | −1.0 |
| Estonia | −8.8 | 5.0 | −4.3 | −2.1 |
| Georgia | −27.5 | 5.2 | −10.8 | 6.9[1] |
| Hungary | −3.3 | 3.6 | −7.2 | 0.4 |
| Kazakhstan | −9.6 | 0.6 | −4.2 | −1.0 |
| Kyrgyzstan | −14.4 | 3.6 | −1.5 | 1.2 |
| Latvia | −15.9 | 3.7 | −6.3 | 0.7 |
| Lithuania | 13.4 | 3.3 | −2.5 | −0.9 |
| Macedonia | −5.5 | 2.2 | −6.0 | −3.9 |
| Moldova | −20.5 | −2.3 | −5.1 | −1.7 |
| Poland | 1.0 | 5.5 | −2.9 | 0.9 |
| Romania | −4.3 | −0.2 | −2.0 | −3.4[2] |
| Russian Federation | −10.3 | 0.2 | −2.3 | −1.0 |
| Slovakia | −5.2 | 4.5 | −3.8 | 0.0 |
| Slovenia | −1.7 | 4.3 | −4.7 | 0.4 |
| Tajikistan | −20.1 | −2.1 | −1.1 | −1.0 |
| Turkmenistan | −9.2 | 3.9 | 3.5 | 2.4 |
| Ukraine | −14.1 | −3.8 | −2.4 | −1.3 |
| Uzbekistan | −4.9 | 3.1 | 1.3 | 1.2 |
| Yugoslavia | −18.0 | 1.4 | −2.8 | −1.3 |
| **Total CSEE** | **−3.1** | **3.2** | **−4.0** | **−0.4[2]** |
| **Total Baltic States** | **−13.3** | **3.8** | **−4.1** | **−1.1** |
| **Total CIS** | **−11.1** | **0.1** | **−2.3** | **−1.1[1]** |

Notes: [1] 1994–98.  [2] 1994–99.

Source: United Nations' Economic Commission for Europe (UNECE) Common Database, authors' calculations.

macroeconomic imbalances, employment declined further (or again). Towards the end of the 1990s, macroeconomic and structural factors had contributed to a new reduction in employment virtually everywhere. Section 2.2 of this chapter discusses various reasons for these developments.

In line with employment losses in the formal economy, all transition countries saw rapid growth in informal employment. The size of its informal economy tends to correlate negatively with the economic level of a country. One reason for expansion in the informal economy is tax evasion, which has been facilitated by legislative changes lagging behind economic developments, and the new legislation's poor enforcement. A second factor is the steep decline in incomes experienced by a major share of the population in connection with the transition crisis and rising unemployment. Economic recovery and progress in legislative reform in Central Europe[5] have been accompanied by some reduction in activity in the informal economy.[6] When formal and informal labour inputs are taken together, employment decline has actually been much smaller than official labour statistics indicate.

The CIS countries, and initially also the Baltic States, faced a slower decline (and some countries even an increase) in employment, despite considerable production losses. These downward trends in employment continued while those of production began to slow and eventually turned, with the result that the CIS countries finally achieved some improvement in labour productivity. However, only very recently have some of these countries enjoyed a slight rise in employment. Moreover, apart from a much larger share of informal labour compared with the CEECA countries,[7] those in the CIS group also show high underemployment (or hidden unemployment, according to some experts in the field) manifested in forced administrative leave,[8] temporary reductions in working hours, and wage payment delays.

---

[5] The Central European countries are the Czech Republic, Hungary, Poland, Slovakia and Slovenia.

[6] In Poland, a 1998 labour force survey on the "hidden" economy revealed that 4.8 per cent of the population aged 15 and over was engaged in the informal economy (3.8 per cent in rural areas and 6.4 per cent in urban areas). Unregistered activity was more frequent in the case of men (7 per cent of the male population aged 15 and over) than women (2.7 per cent). Regarding their official labour market status, 5.5 per cent of workers engaged in informal activities were employed, 14.6 per cent were unemployed and 2.4 per cent economically inactive. For 14 per cent of respondents, this was a permanent activity carried out for five months or more, while for 30 per cent it represented only up to five days. Compared with the results of a similar survey conducted in 1995, a significant decrease in unregistered labour was observed. The share of persons aged 15 and over engaged in the informal economy dropped by 2.8 percentage points, from 7.6 per cent in 1995 to 4.8 per cent in 1998. This decline is mainly attributable to a general improvement in the labour market during this period, with more job opportunities emerging in the formal economy. See Kostrubiec (1999).

[7] For the Russian Federation the estimates of the share of workers involved in the informal economy differ widely. Clarke (1998) estimated the share of informal employment performed as a main activity at 5 per cent of total employment in 1997, and 10 per cent of the employed population to be informally employed in a second job. A household survey conducted by the All-Russia Centre for Public Opinion, by contrast, put the level of informal employment conducted as a main activity at 11.6 per cent of total employment in 1997 (Ministry of Labour and Social Development of the Russian Federation, 1998).

[8] Administrative leave is the name given to enforced unpaid leave at the request of management, in order to temporarily reduce production and its related labour costs.

## 2.1.2 Shrinking participation rates

Employment losses were transformed partly into open unemployment and partly into (formal) economic inactivity. Indeed, according to table 2.2, participation rates of the population aged 15–64 declined considerably in all the transition countries between 1990 and 1999 (with the striking exception of almost negligible changes in Georgia and Slovenia). A comparison of employment outflow in five transition countries, using labour market flow data from labour force surveys, reveals that outflows to inactivity have generally exceeded outflows to unemployment (see table 4.10 in Chapter 4, where the results are discussed in more detail). This imbalance was marked in the initial period of economic transition, indicating that strong labour market tensions were resolved primarily by pushing certain disadvantaged, less competitive groups of workers out of the labour market – and only secondarily resolved by open unemployment.

This decline in participation rates is often explained in the literature by more frequent withdrawals of women from the labour market as a result of their deteriorating access to affordable and reliable childcare facilities and the offer of long parental leave (notwithstanding a generally low parental allowance). To this argument is added the allegedly higher labour costs of women, and their family status as second-income earner, both of which might influence their decision to resign from formal gainful activity. However, table 2.2 confirms this view for only seven countries (Armenia, Bulgaria, the Czech Republic, Estonia, Latvia, Macedonia and Slovakia); in all others, participation rates declined more for men than for women or the decline was similar.

Table 2.3 compares the participation rates for three age groups: young (15–24), prime-age (25–49) and older (50–64) workers in selected transition economies. The steepest fall in labour supply is found in the 15–24 age group, many of whom are extending their studies into higher education before joining the labour market. A second factor explaining these low rates is the increasingly difficult transition from education to work. Employers are unwilling to bear the additional costs of on-the-job training for inexperienced young workers; and here an insider/outsider effect may also play a significant role (for more on this effect, see Chapter 5). In addition, many young people are confronted with a lack of demand for their newly gained professional education as a consequence of unsatisfactory reforms to the national education systems, which lag considerably behind labour market needs and lead to skill mismatches and employers' complaints of low quality of education.

For older workers, the comparison is somewhat ambiguous. At the start of the transition, working pensioners were the first group to be laid off everywhere; many countries introduced early retirement schemes to avoid the long-term unemployment of older workers. This approach has recently changed. First, early retirement schemes have been reduced or even discontinued because they heavily burdened national pension systems already in deficit. Second, in order to make pension systems more financially sustainable, the statutory retirement age has been raised in many transition countries. Third, low pension levels force older workers to keep working and accept worse jobs, while an improved labour market situation has also

**11**

Table 2.2   Participation rates of population aged 15–64, transition economies, 1990 and 1999 (percentages)

| Country | 1990 | | | 1999 | | |
|---|---|---|---|---|---|---|
| | Men | Women | Total | Men | Women | Total |
| Albania[a] | 86.4 | 63.3 | 75.2 | .. | .. | .. |
| Armenia[ab] | 79.5 | 69.1 | 74.1 | 78.5[1] | 55.6[1] | 66.4[2] |
| Azerbaijan[ac] | 77.8 | 36.4 | 66.7 | 50.1[2] | 44.2[2] | 47.1[2] |
| Belarus[ac] | 82.0 | 72.6 | 77.2 | 45.8[2] | 46.0[2] | 45.9[2] |
| Bulgaria[a] | 77.7 | 72.2 | 75.0 | 75.9 | 64.9 | 70.2 |
| Croatia[ab] | 76.9 | 56.4 | 66.6 | 59.8[2] | 51.4[2] | 55.6[2] |
| Czech Republic[ab] | 82.2 | 74.1 | 78.1 | 80.3 | 64.4 | 72.4 |
| Estonia[ab] | 83.3 | 75.9 | 79.4 | 78.1 | 66.4 | 72.1 |
| Georgia[ab] | 80.1 | 63.5 | 71.5 | 78.9 | 62.5 | 70.2 |
| Hungary[bd] | 74.5 | 57.3 | 65.4 | 67.8 | 52.3 | 59.9 |
| Kazakhstan[e] | 82.0[4] | 69.5[4] | 75.6[4] | .. | .. | .. |
| Kyrgyzstan[e] | 78.2[4] | 65.0[4] | 71.5[4] | .. | .. | .. |
| Latvia[ab] | 83.6 | 75.3 | 79.4 | 75.3 | 62.6 | 68.7 |
| Lithuania[ac] | 81.8 | 70.5 | 76.0 | 77.4 | 68.3 | 72.7 |
| Macedonia[ab] | 77.9 | 53.1 | 65.6 | 72.8 | 46.5 | 59.7 |
| Moldova[a] | 81.5 | 70.4 | 75.7 | .. | .. | .. |
| Poland[ab] | 80.1 | 65.1 | 72.5 | 72.8 | 59.7 | 66.1 |
| Romania[ab] | 76.7 | 60.5 | 68.5 | 76.3[2] | 61.9[2] | 69.0[2] |
| Russian Fed.[ab] | 91.6 | 71.7 | 76.5 | 74.2 | 63.9 | 68.9 |
| Slovakia[ab] | 82.5 | 74.2 | 78.3 | 76.1 | 62.6 | 69.3 |
| Slovenia[ab] | 76.7 | 64.8 | 70.7 | 72.2 | 63.3 | 68.0 |
| Tajikistan[ac] | 77.7 | 56.2 | 66.8 | 32.5[5] | 28.2[5] | 30.3[5] |
| Turkmenistan[a] | 81.0 | 64.3 | 72.5 | .. | .. | .. |
| Ukraine[ab] | 79.7 | 69.8 | 74.5 | 71.4 | 61.8 | 66.4 |
| Uzbekistan[a] | 77.9 | 64.2 | 71.0 | .. | .. | .. |
| Yugoslavia[a] | 77.0 | 54.9 | 66.0 | .. | .. | .. |

Notes: [1] 1997. [2] 1998, ages 15+. [3] 1998. [4] 1989. [5] 1996, ages 15+.  .. = not available.

Sources: Authors' calculations based on: [a] Economically active population, ILO, Bureau of Statistics (data for 1990); [b] Labour force survey; [c] Official estimates; [d] Establishment census; [e] Population census.

Table 2.3   Participation rates according to age group, transition economies, 1990 and 1999 (percentages)

| Country | 1990 Age group | | | 1999 Age group | | |
|---|---|---|---|---|---|---|
| | 15–24 | 25–49 | 50–64 | 15–24 | 25–49 | 50–64 |
| Albania[a] | 59.5 | 87.7 | 64.4 | .. | .. | .. |
| Armenia[ab] | 49.7 | 90.9 | 61.3 | 27.3[1] | 85.3[1] | 64.7[1] |
| Azerbaijan[ac] | 48.8 | 85.8 | 56.3 | .. | .. | .. |
| Belarus[ac] | 52.4 | 96.1 | 60.2 | .. | .. | .. |
| Bulgaria[a] | 51.9 | 95.1 | 55.3 | .. | .. | .. |
| Croatia[ab] | 45.8 | 86.8* | 43.5** | 40.3[2] | 70.5[2]* | 23.3[2]** |
| Czech Republic[ab] | 57.7 | 96.0 | 55.7 | 48.7 | 89.3 | 59.4 |
| Estonia[ab] | 53.0 | 95.6 | 68.5 | 43.5 | 88.2 | 62.2 |
| Georgia[ab] | 47.3 | 85.7 | 65.4 | 37.2 | 80.4 | 75.0 |
| Hungary[bd] | 51.5 | 86.0 | 36.0 | 40.7 | 79.0 | 37.9 |
| Kazakhstan[e] | 53.8[3] | 93.9[3] | 55.7[3] | .. | .. | .. |
| Kyrgyzstan[e] | 50.5[3] | 92.3[3] | 50.9[3] | .. | .. | .. |
| Latvia[ab] | 56.1 | 95.1 | 67.4 | 41.6 | 87.0 | 53.1 |
| Lithuania[ac] | 49.5 | 93.9 | 61.9 | 39.8 | 92.6 | 59.8 |
| Macedonia[ab] | 44.5 | 81.4 | 49.5 | 38.8 | 76.6 | 42.1 |
| Moldova[a] | 53.0 | 94.9 | 52.4 | .. | .. | .. |
| Poland[ab] | 44.3 | 87.3 | 60.6 | 37.3 | 85.0 | 47.8 |
| Romania[ab] | 59.8 | 87.7 | 42.9 | 45.8[2] | 84.8[2] | 58.1[2] |
| Russian Federation[ab] | 52.4 | 95.2 | 57.7 | 41.9 | 87.7 | 48.8 |
| Slovakia[ab] | 58.8 | 95.6 | 55.3 | 45.6 | 89.5 | 45.6 |
| Slovenia[ab] | 50.4 | 93.1 | 42.0 | 41.8 | 91.3 | 38.2 |
| Tajikistan[ac] | 49.1 | 84.5 | 53.0 | .. | .. | .. |
| Turkmenistan[a] | 56.2 | 88.9 | 56.1 | .. | .. | .. |
| Ukraine[ab] | 51.5 | 94.7 | 55.5 | 42.1 | 86.0 | 46.0 |
| Uzbekistan[a] | 52.5 | 90.0 | 51.4 | .. | .. | .. |
| Yugoslavia[a] | 45.1 | 84.9 | 46.6 | .. | .. | .. |

Notes:  [1] 1997. [2] 1998. [3] 1989. * Ages 25–54. ** Ages 55–64. .. = not available.

Sources:  Authors' calculations based on: [a] Economically active population, ILO, Bureau of Statistics (data for 1990); [b] Labour force survey; [c] Official estimates; [d] Establishment census; [e] Population census.

opened job opportunities for less competitive groups of workers. For all these reasons, participation rates for the 50–64 age group tended to recover in the second half of the 1990s – to such an extent that Armenia, the Czech Republic, Hungary, Georgia and Romania have recorded an overall increase over the past decade. Still, in Macedonia, Poland and Ukraine the 50–64 group showed the highest decline in economic activity. In five other countries (Latvia, Lithuania, the Russian Federation, Slovakia and Slovenia), the 50–64-year-olds ranked second among the three age groups (see table 2.3).

The reasons for these considerable declines in economic activity (even in the prime-age 25–49 group most typically represented in employment) are numerous. They include voluntary withdrawals (for example, people who had their previously nationalized property returned to them; or the spouses of leading executives and entrepreneurs), semi-voluntary quits (for example, women on extended maternity or parental leave[9]), or forced withdrawals (discouraged workers, including those who opt for social welfare combined with informal work instead of accepting low-paid or arduous jobs).

## 2.1.3  Unemployment trends

As noted earlier, open unemployment has been the second main destination of workers unable to find new employment after voluntarily quitting or being made redundant. Once again, a major difference in the level and development trends of unemployment is observed between the two groups of transition countries.

In the CSEE countries, with the exception of the Czech Republic and partly also Romania, registered unemployment accelerated in the first two to three years after the introduction of economic reforms, reaching double-digit levels in most countries by 1994 (table 2.4). Economic recovery contributed first to the stabilization of the unemployment rate and only later to its slight decline, supported in part by restrictions in national unemployment benefit schemes, which will be discussed further in section 2.2.5. Slumps in economic performance, followed by macroeconomic stabilization programmes launched with the aim of restoring macroeconomic equilibrium and pushing structural reforms in the enterprise sector in some countries (Bulgaria, the Czech Republic and Romania), led to a second rise in unemployment after 1997 (or 1998), this time also heavily hitting the Czech Republic. After 1998, structural reforms also accelerated in other CSEE countries (some in connection with the progress in EU accession negotiations), with a similar effect of a rise in unemployment. In those countries directly affected by war or conflict, unemployment levels have risen considerably higher.

Another characteristic of some countries in the CSEE group is an excess of registered unemployment over unemployment measured by labour force survey (LFS)

---

[9] As parental allowances are low, a large number of these women would prefer to work if they had access to cheap and reliable childcare and could get a well-paid job.

Table 2.4   Registered unemployment (as a percentage of labour force at end of each year), transition economies, 1994, 1998 and 2000

| Country | 1994 | 1998 | 2000 |
|---|---|---|---|
| Albania | 18.0 | 17.6 | 16.9 |
| Armenia | 6.0 | 8.9 | 10.9 |
| Azerbaijan | 0.9 | 1.4 | 1.2 |
| Belarus | 2.1 | 2.3 | 2.1 |
| Bulgaria | 12.8 | 12.2 | 17.9 |
| Croatia | 17.3 | 18.6 | 22.6 |
| Czech Republic | 3.2 | 7.5 | 8.8 |
| Estonia[1] | 5.0 | 4.5 | 6.6 |
| Georgia | 3.8 | 4.2 | 5.6[2] |
| Hungary | 10.9 | 9.1 | 8.9 |
| Kazakhstan | 1.0 | 3.7 | 3.7 |
| Kyrgyzstan | 0.8 | 3.1 | 3.1 |
| Latvia | 6.5 | 9.2 | 7.8 |
| Lithuania | 4.5 | 6.9 | 12.6 |
| Macedonia | 30.0 | 41.4 | 44.9 |
| Moldova | 1.0 | 1.9 | 1.8 |
| Poland | 16.4 | 10.4 | 15.1 |
| Romania | 10.9 | 10.3 | 10.5 |
| Russian Federation | 2.1 | 2.7 | 1.4 |
| Slovakia | 14.8 | 15.6 | 17.9 |
| Slovenia | 14.2 | 14.6 | 12.0 |
| Tajikistan | 1.8 | 2.9 | 3.0 |
| Ukraine | 0.3 | 4.3 | 4.2 |
| Yugoslavia | 14.2 | 14.6 | 12.0[3] |

Notes: [1] Jobseekers. [2] 1999. [3] excluding Kosovo and Metohia.

Source: UNECE, 2001, p. 167. For Estonia, Labour Market Board data.

data (compare table 2.4 with table 2.5). This difference is sensitive to changes in incentives for unemployment registration. In the Czech Republic, Poland and Slovakia the extent of this over-registration was limited, and mostly disappeared with cuts in unemployment benefit systems. However, in Croatia, Hungary, Romania and Slovenia it has persisted, pinpointing a certain level of misuse of public welfare schemes.

Table 2.5    Total unemployment, selected transition countries, 1994, 1998 and 2000

| Country | 1994 | 1998 | 2000 |
|---|---|---|---|
| Armenia[a] | .. | 36.4[1] | .. |
| Bulgaria[a] | 20.2 | 14.4[1] | 18.7 |
| Croatia[a] | 10.0[2] | 11.4 | 13.5[3] |
| Czech Republic[a] | 4.3 | 7.3 | 8.8 |
| Estonia[a] | 7.6 | 9.9 | 13.5 |
| Georgia[a] | .. | 14.5 | 13.8[3] |
| Hungary[a] | 10.7 | 7.8 | 6.6 |
| Kazakhstan[b] | 7.5 | 13.7 | .. |
| Latvia[a] | 18.9[4] | 13.8 | 14.4 |
| Lithuania[a] | 16.4[2] | 13.3 | 15.9 |
| Poland[a] | 14.0 | 10.5 | 16.6 |
| Romania[b] | 8.2 | 6.3 | 7.7 |
| Russian Federation[a] | 8.1 | 13.3 | 13.4[3] |
| Slovakia[a] | 13.7 | 12.5 | 19.1 |
| Slovenia[a] | 9.0 | 7.7 | 7.1 |
| Ukraine[a] | 5.6[4] | 11.3 | 11.9[3] |

Notes: [1] 1997. [2] 1996. [3] 1999. [4] 1995.

Sources: [a] Labour force survey. [b] Official estimates.

The CIS countries have been characterized by a slower but persistent growth in unemployment measured by LFS data and by very low levels of registered unemployment (tables 2.4 and 2.5). The LFS levels are now above 10 per cent and in the conflict countries considerably higher, but they are still relatively low compared with the huge production losses in these countries. Economic recovery recently achieved by the Russian Federation has led to a decline in open unemployment.

The low level of registered unemployment relative to LFS-measured total unemployment in the CIS countries (between 1998 and 2000 even decreasing in a number of them) is mainly attributable to the unwillingness of public labour market institutions to provide meaningful assistance to unemployed persons, primarily because of a shortage of funds. Eligibility rules for registration as a jobseeker are set in such a way that many jobseekers do not qualify. Jobs reported to public employment services (PES) are usually of poor quality and unattractive for more competitive jobseekers, who rely on other channels of job-finding. The range of active labour market programmes and the number of jobs on offer are limited. The average level of unemployment benefits is also very low, except for the few who are formally made redundant. Frequent budgetary problems cause benefits to be paid irregularly. In addition, understaffing and low salaries do not motivate PES employees to provide high-quality re-employment assistance to jobseekers.

The larger discrepancy between registered unemployment and LFS data also remains typical for the three Baltic transition countries. In the second half of the 1990s registered unemployment accelerated due to labour market policy changes in eligibility criteria, so that both unemployment indicators have edged closer.

## 2.1.4  Characteristics of unemployment

### *Long-term unemployment on the rise*

A troubling aspect of unemployment in the transition countries is its long-term nature. According to LFS data, the share of long-term unemployment (over one year) in total unemployment in 1999 exceeded 40 per cent in most countries (with the puzzling exception of 22 per cent for Lithuania) and climbed to 68 per cent in Armenia. Recently, more countries have succeeded in some reduction of long-term joblessness, but in the Czech Republic, Estonia and the Russian Federation it has increased considerably (respectively from 31 per cent, 33 per cent and 30 per cent in 1995 to 49 per cent, 47 per cent and 41 per cent in 2000), indicating the existence of particular groups of unemployed persons with a minimal chance of re-employment. These groups usually combine several disadvantages (low skills, higher age, immobility, health problems, or employer prejudice), making their placement difficult even after retraining or participation in temporary employment programmes. Their problems increase with longer unemployment spells and need to be tackled more straightforwardly – a need often impeded by the shortage of public funds. An improved labour market situation can offer them a better chance of re-employment.

### *Unemployment by age*

Young people, in particular school leavers with no work experience, are the group hardest hit by unemployment, despite the sharp decline in their participation rates described earlier. In most transition countries, unemployment rates of young people under the age of 25 are at least twice the national average, as table 2.6 shows. As a rule, the incidence of unemployment tends to decline with age, reaching the lowest levels for the pre-retirement population. This is related to persisting seniority rules and insiders' power, especially in large enterprises, and the frequent willingness of older workers to accept worse jobs. It is also partly related to early retirement, pre-retirement arrangements or disability pensions often offered to older workers who are either threatened by redundancy or who are already jobless.

### *A gender perspective on unemployment levels*

For women, perceived by employers as less competitive workers due to child-raising or care responsibilities, the situation is again ambiguous. Registered unemployment

Table 2.6    Youth total (LFS) unemployment rate, selected transition economies,
2000 (percentages)

| Country | Youth unemployment rate (population aged 15–24) | National average unemployment rate (population aged 15–64) |
|---|---|---|
| Bulgaria | 9.4 | 18.7 |
| Czech Republic | 17.0 | 8.8 |
| Estonia | 23.7 | 13.5 |
| Hungary | 12.3 | 6.6 |
| Latvia | 21.2 | 14.4 |
| Lithuania | 27.5 | 15.9 |
| Macedonia | 59.9 | 32.5 |
| Poland | 35.7 | 16.6 |
| Romania | 17.8 | 7.7 |
| Slovakia | 36.9 | 19.1 |
| Slovenia | 16.4 | 7.1 |

Source: Eurostat, 2001.

data clearly show higher unemployment levels for women in all transition countries with the exception of Hungary. However, the picture becomes more diverse for LFS unemployment, with rates higher for men than for women in Armenia, Georgia, Hungary, Lithuania, the Russian Federation and Ukraine, while in Bulgaria and Romania the levels are almost the same. This disparity is primarily explained by the higher reliance of women on job-search facilities and income support assistance from the PES. It also reflects a greater willingness among women to take up low-paid, precarious jobs in the public sector, in unprofitable enterprises, or in newly created jobs with small private firms, particularly in the service sector.

## Disadvantaged groups

Low-skilled workers are also more affected by unemployment. The probability of unemployment incidence declines with the increasing level of education (although in some countries people with blue-collar vocational training face even more severe unemployment problems than those with no skills[10]). People with disabilities or health problems, and ethnic minorities perceived by some employers as "unskilled" and

---

[10] The previous narrow specialization of blue-collar vocational professions often makes transfer to other industries (or agriculture) problematic, especially to industries already undergoing transition shrinkage. Higher age groups, with less access (and often less willingness) to retrain, are most affected.

"unreliable" workers (for example, people from the Roma community), have an extremely high incidence of unemployment, "solved" by many through inactivity.

## 2.1.5 Regional disparities in unemployment

Aside from high aggregate unemployment, the transition countries experience large regional disparities in unemployment, increasing from county to district level and from district to community level. This springs from the past legacy of a high concentration of production in large enterprises, often the main job providers for an entire region: as these enterprises collapse, regional unemployment climbs. A second factor is the low mobility of the population, which paradoxically has further declined in the course of transition. Given that attachment to domicile and a localized social network is characteristic of most of Europe, the even lower mobility in transition countries has been compounded by the privatization of state-owned or cooperative houses and flats. Home ownership has strengthened ties to locality. In addition, public transport fares have increased considerably and many transport connections discontinued after public or enterprise subsidies were withdrawn. Petrol prices have also risen; thus, even if they own a car, many people cannot afford to commute to work. At the current low level of wages, many who previously commuted have ceased to do so.

The costs of housing also differ considerably by region and have become prohibitive for less competitive workers, who are obliged to stay put in regions with high unemployment, while competitive workers have access to jobs anywhere. Gradually, the quality of the labour supply in depressed regions deteriorates further. This severely limits the prospects for improving regional disparities in unemployment, unless the situation is corrected by a carefully designed regional policy targeting both the supply and demand sides of the labour market.

The above analysis of the trends and structure of unemployment shows that, in the process of transformation, the character of unemployment has changed. In the initial period, unemployment was clearly transitional in character, mainly influenced by the extraordinary depth of the transition crisis and the extent of accumulated labour hoarding. However, it was soon transformed into structural unemployment, as reflected in the very high level of long-term unemployment – associated with chronic weak aggregate demand for labour and wide regional disparities in employability triggered by immobility, inflexibility or a lack of skills – persisting even once the economy recovered.

In the CSEE countries, the level of frictional unemployment is relatively modest due, among other reasons, to well-developed information channels, including the PES systems which function more effectively than their counterparts in CIS countries. Cyclical unemployment is also present in periods of economic downturns, but is less relevant. Understanding the nature of unemployment is very important for the adequate formulation of labour market policies. Unfortunately, this has not often been the case during the past decade.

In addition to the characteristics and developments addressed above, the next section explores other pertinent factors affecting cross-country differences in the labour market performance of the CSEE and the CIS transition economies.

## 2.2 FACTORS CONTRIBUTING TO CROSS-COUNTRY DIFFERENCES IN LABOUR MARKET DEVELOPMENT IN TRANSITION COUNTRIES

### 2.2.1 Economic and social conditions on the starting line of transition

From the outset of their political, economic and social transformation, considerable differences existed among the transition economies that were disregarded until recently by many Western scholars. First, the CSEE countries were able to benefit from their past experience and more frequent trade contacts with world markets. The shift from Eastern to Western markets was easier and less painful for domestic enterprises in these countries. Territorial proximity also played a leading role for the CSEE countries in finding new external markets for domestic products, helping to preserve more jobs and promising new job openings after economic recovery. In contrast, the shift for non-Russian CIS countries was extremely difficult because within the framework of the Soviet Union the limited foreign trade that existed had been exclusively controlled by Moscow.

Second, a number of CSEE countries had retained a limited private sector (almost exclusively in the form of self-employment) under the previous regime.[11] Clearly, the CSEE countries were benefiting from their pre-communist industrial and entrepreneurial tradition, a past that was much more remote for the CIS countries. This advantage reduced risk-aversion in many potential CSEE entrepreneurs who wished to tap into newly emerging market opportunities, and stimulated job creation in newly established firms.

Third, the countries differed in their inherited external and internal imbalances. Heavily indebted countries, such as Hungary and Poland, had to spend a larger share of public finance on debt servicing, constraining their economic and social interventions, compared with those countries with low levels of debt such as Bulgaria or the former Czechoslovakia. As the Russian Federation took over almost the entire Soviet Union's external debt, the majority of other ex-Soviet countries started their transition without any external debt at all. The varying levels of suppressed inflation (low in Hungary and Czechoslovakia and high, in particular, in the CIS countries and Bulgaria) and the distortions in relative prices (Hungary was an early starter in correcting for price distortions) were immediately reflected in the scale of price increases after price liberalization and were later responsible for the depth of the transition crisis and a decline in labour demand.

Fourth, variations in the age structure and the quality of labour supply were also telling. Compared with non-transition countries at a similar economic level, the average educational level of the labour force was high. Nevertheless, significant differences also existed. These included higher shares of workers with primary or

---

[11] For more information, see Chapter 3, section 3.2.

lower education in non Central European countries compared with Central European ones; very strong secondary education (especially technical) in the Czech Republic, for example; and different proportions of tertiary education in various transition countries. These differences denoted the capacity and speed of countries to adjust production to changing market demands, to attract foreign investors and to upgrade workforce skills to new labour market needs.

Fifth, the former republics of the Soviet Union, as well as the ex-Yugoslav countries and Slovakia, lacked experience in operating as independent economies. They were confronted with the task of introducing a new own currency, establishing a new independent banking system and other institutions, finding new energy resources, and so forth, on top of the transition tasks common to all post-communist countries.

## 2.2.2 The role of economic policy

All the transition countries embarked on the same three postulates advised by the Washington Consensus[12] – namely, privatization, price and trade liberalization and macroeconomic stabilization – but varied widely in their pace, extent and modes of implementation. For example, although Poland was very fast in almost complete liberalization of prices combined with currency devaluation and strict macro-economic austerity measures (only gradually relaxed after 1991), it was slow in privatization and the structural reform of certain sectors (agriculture, coal mining, steel). This stance helped Poland to overcome the transition crisis speedily and embark on high economic growth, but created increasing structural problems and economic imbalances. These were tackled by a tight monetary policy and acceleration of structural changes after 1998. At the same time Poland introduced four major reforms (to the pension system, the territorial administrative system, health care and education). The combination of the strict monetary policy, large-scale structural changes and major social reforms with many initial problems and deficiencies, alongside negative external shocks, has resulted in a significant economic slowdown and escalating unemployment.

Hungary benefited from its advanced position in price and trade liberalization and concentrated on the restructuring and privatization of enterprises, relying mainly on direct sales. It also encouraged foreign direct investment (FDI) through economic incentives. Nevertheless, the loose monetary and fiscal policy accelerated macroeconomic imbalances that necessitated a strict stabilization policy package in 1995. A serious economic slowdown ensued, with further cuts in labour demand. Pro-active economic policy launched after 1997 clearly stimulated rapid economic recovery, eventually leading to limited employment growth and reduced unemployment.

---

[12] John Williamson first coined this term in 1990 (Williamson, 1990), referring to what he considered "the lowest common denominator of policy advice", including privatization, tight fiscal and monetary policies, and freer trade and capital flows, being addressed by the Washington-based institutions to the Latin American countries. We refer here to United States economic officials, the International Monetary Fund, and the World Bank advising the transition countries in the early years of change.

In contrast, the Czech Republic opted for almost complete price and foreign trade liberalization and steep devaluation of its currency, while relying on voucher privatization[13] and the restructuring of those enterprises with strong ties to domestic state-owned banks. This policy, initially successful in promoting structural changes in the economy at a relatively low social cost, gradually led to increasing macroeconomic imbalances, the heavy indebtedness of many enterprises and the virtual collapse of the banking sector. An austerity policy package introduced in 1997 resulted in economic recession, escalating lay-offs and open unemployment. Recovery was achieved only in 2000.

These three examples of Central European countries, considered (along with Estonia, Slovakia and Slovenia) as the most advanced in economic transition, illustrate the prominent role that economic policy plays in determining the structure and level of labour demand, and hence employment and unemployment. Since each country implemented its own approach, intrinsically dependent on its prevailing political climate and conditions, it is difficult to make any valid generalizations. The commitment of national governments to economic reform and sound economic policies has exerted a strong influence on subsequent economic and labour market developments in some countries. However, in those countries with adverse starting conditions (the weight of their communist past, isolation from foreign markets, greater economic imbalances), it has been far harder to maintain the pace of reform – unless, like Estonia, they have been able to benefit from their small size, a favourable popular mentality and strong external assistance.

For most countries, the severe social consequences for the population, coupled with an understandable ignorance of the sum effects of certain systemic and policy changes and, often, cronyism, led to many inconsistencies in the reform process. In turn, this contributed to intensifying negative outcomes and the postponement of economic and labour market recovery. One concrete example of reform inconsistency is the frequently cited delay in institutional reforms in CIS countries. This slow progress impeded enterprise restructuring, further weakened the banking system, undermined economic growth and eventually led to mounting internal and external instability and economic crisis.

The combination of a country's starting conditions, internal factors (the speed and consistency of economic reforms, orientation of economic policy vis-à-vis economic growth promotion, and the proximity to new solvent markets) and external factors (such as the impact of war or conflict and recession of their main trading partners) is responsible for most differences in the economic performance of transition countries. As clearly reflected in varying labour market developments, the Central European countries – the Czech Republic, Hungary, Poland, Slovakia and Slovenia – were more successful in returning to economic growth fairly quickly, followed by Croatia, Estonia, Latvia and Lithuania. Bulgaria and Romania were able to catch up only later.

---

[13] A book of vouchers costing CZK1000 was made available for purchase to every Czech citizen over the age of 18. The vouchers could then be traded for shares in designated state-owned enterprises. The vouchers were released in two rounds.

Most recently, the CIS countries have finally returned to economic growth albeit from rather low levels. Nevertheless, so far only four countries, with Poland in first place, recently followed by Slovenia, Slovakia and Hungary, have been able to exceed their pre-transition levels.

Through a cross-country comparison, the employment effects of privatization of large enterprises, inflow of foreign direct investment and small enterprise development are analysed in the following chapter.

## 2.2.3 Legal and institutional reforms

While all the transition countries made legislative amendments and restructured institutions to conform to the market system, progress has been unequal and has generated observable differences. The reasons for this unequal development have been many: legal experts unfamiliar with the functioning of a market system; ideological expectations that the State should withdraw from the enterprise sector and its macroeconomic environment as much as possible (in the belief that free-market forces would cure all ills); the misjudgement of international advisers in under-estimating institutional reforms while emphasizing one-sided economic reforms; political instability impeding the progress of legal and institutional reforms; cronyism; and the determined opposition of some politicians and "new rich" to the introduction of legislation to curtail profiteering from the privatization of state property. In the Czech Republic, for example, the inadequate protection of small shareholders in mass privatization was the direct consequence of a weak legal environment, seriously damaging the only advantage of voucher privatization – its original fairness for the populace.[14]

The perception by Western investors of the weak legal protection of property rights in many transition economies, in particular the CIS, was the main reason for the slow inflow of FDI to these countries, despite promisingly high returns. The 1998 *Economic Survey of Europe* undertaken by the United Nations Economic Commission for Europe (UNECE, 1998) advanced strong arguments that the Russian financial crisis of August 1998 was the result of poor economic restructuring and adjustment of the enterprise sector, caused (among other factors) by a weak institutional framework. It concluded that any macroeconomic stabilization without deep structural and behavioural changes in the enterprise sector, backed up and stimulated by appropriate institutional reforms, would be unsustainable and short-lived (UNECE, 1998, p. 12). In contrast, improvements in legislation and strengthening of market institutions in the process of the EU accession are behind the recently accelerating FDI inflows in Central Europe. Reforms to labour market institutions and their impact on the labour market situation are evaluated below.

---

[14] A theoretical assumption – in practice, people had unequal access to information both on the actual economic situation and the market price of the enterprises participating in voucher privatization.

## 2.2.4  Labour supply factors

*Demographic factors*

The labour market situation has also been considerably affected by demographic changes. The 1990s, in particular the first half, were characterized by a strong entry of young people between 15 and 25 years old.[15] This coincided with significant changes in the demand for skills and the depreciation of work experience due to massive restructuring in the CSEE (much less so in the CIS), which favoured young, skilled workers. However, after the initial wave of restructuring, employers shifted to a renewed preference for prime-age workers with work experience. As noted earlier, lagging national educational reforms have responded inadequately to changing labour market needs; often schools and training centres are not supplying the education demanded by the market. As job creation still remains low, school leavers without work experience are increasingly confronted with unemployment, and some have responded by staying longer in education.

Another demographic factor of significance in the transition countries is a sharp decline in fertility rates. Reasons include the falling incomes of young families, housing problems faced by young people and women's fear of job loss (because of child-raising). New career opportunities opening up for women are also a factor in lower fertility rates. In the short term, the consequence is fewer women on maternity/ parental leave; in the long term, it will contribute to a more rapid ageing of the population.

In the initial years of economic transition, non Central European transition countries also experienced an increase in mortality and morbidity rates, explained by a declining expenditure on health care as a result of state budget cuts and shrinking incomes. There is also a rising health problem in these countries posed by the elevated levels of stress caused by unemployment and poverty.[16] This may be one cause of the substantial growth in disability pensions among older workers: the other, more importantly, is the "solving" of labour market problems of older workers, especially those with poorer health, by offering them disability pensions.

*Effects of education*

Table 2.7 shows the high average levels of education among the population aged 15–64 in selected transition countries. Although cross-country comparisons of education levels are imprecise because of wide variations in national education systems, there are substantial differences between countries in the proportion of population with only

---

[15] In Poland, unlike many other transition countries, the proportion of persons aged between 15 and 24 in the total population increased constantly over the whole decade. This is often cited as one explanation for accelerating unemployment after 1997 and an exceptionally high youth unemployment rate (more than double the national average).

[16] For more on this aspect, see Cornia and Paniccià (2000). In this connection, a massive drop in the life expectancy of males in the Russian Federation, from 64.2 years in 1989 to 57.6 years in 1994, is often cited. Although life expectancy recovered in all the transition countries after 1995, in many of them it still remains below pre-transition levels.

Table 2.7   Composition of population, aged 15–64, according to education level, selected transition economies, 2000 (percentage of total population)

| Country | Level of education | | |
|---|---|---|---|
| | Primary* | Secondary** | Tertiary |
| Bulgaria | 43.9 | 42.7 | 13.4 |
| Czech Republic | 23.8 | 67.0 | 9.1 |
| Estonia | 26.2 | 51.3 | 22.5 |
| Hungary | 38.5 | 50.3 | 11.2 |
| Latvia | 30.6 | 55.3 | 14.1 |
| Lithuania | 31.3 | 36.8 | 31.9 |
| Poland | 33.1 | 58.3 | 8.6 |
| Romania | 43.2 | 49.9 | 6.9 |
| Slovakia | 28.8 | 63.5 | 7.6 |
| Slovenia | 33.9 | 53.9 | 12.1 |

Note: * 8–9 years of education. ** 3–4 years of education.

Source: Eurostat, 2001.

primary education, which, for example, is very low in the Czech Republic and Estonia but much higher in Bulgaria and Romania. Since 1990, the proportion of children quitting compulsory primary education early (the minimum school leaving age is between 14 and 16 in most transition countries), or those not progressing to post-compulsory schooling, has increased significantly, in particular in non Central European transition countries. Ethnic minority children and children from poor families are over-represented among early school leavers, pointing to growing social stratification of education, contributing to widening labour market inequalities (see UNICEF, 2001). Low-skilled workers face the greatest problems in the labour market, owing to their restricted ability to adjust to new technologies and new methods of work organization, and this is even more true for young dropouts. Similarly, large cross-country differences are found in the share of population with secondary education, which is very high in the Czech Republic, Slovakia and Poland. Tertiary education levels, by contrast, are considerably higher in Lithuania and Estonia than in the other transition countries. If supported by favourable human resources development, this signals significant potential for growth for these two countries.

The traditional, extremely narrow specialization in vocational education that distinguishes the transition countries has left a legacy of a large share of blue-collar workers with obsolete skills – a problem that has emerged across the board and been dealt with inadequately everywhere. Adult education is insufficiently developed, not only in the training of unemployed jobseekers, which covers only a fraction of those in need of skills upgrading, but also in training those workers threatened by unemployment or who need to upgrade their skills to work with new technologies. Under the previous regime, enterprises delivered training to their staff. New, hard budget constraints have forced many enterprises to close down these facilities and look for skilled workers in the labour market, instead of investing in their own workers.

## 2.2.5  The role of labour market institutions and policies

National labour legislation was substantially and repeatedly amended during the transition to a market system. The objective was to facilitate workforce adjustment for firms, in order to make enterprises more flexible and economically competitive, while guaranteeing solid employment protection for workers. Under the previous centrally planned system, workers enjoyed a fairly high degree of employment protection. The amended employment protection legislation (EPL) substantially moderates workers' protection, both in employment and in the case of redundancy. The overall effect of these legislative changes on employment and unemployment – in general and in regard to specific social groups – will be thoroughly analysed in Chapters 5 and 6.

Labour market policy (LMP) is applied to facilitate the transfer of workers between jobs and between employment, unemployment and inactivity, and to balance labour supply with demand. In all transition countries, LMP (active and passive) was introduced in tandem with economic and social reforms. Unemployment benefit systems were originally set rather generously, in terms of both eligibility rules and the amount and payment duration of benefits, under the assumption of the transitory character of unemployment. When unemployment rates accelerated rapidly and remained high, the rules and benefit levels became considerably more restrictive, in order to economize on limited resources and "activate" jobseekers to take up new jobs.[17]

### Passive LMP

The coverage of registered jobseekers by income support and the average replacement rates of unemployment benefits are analysed in detail in Chapter 6 (see table 6.1). In general, the share of benefit recipients among registered jobseekers is rather low, moving between 23 and 49 per cent for the CEECA countries in 1998, the year for which we have the most complete data. The higher shares for the CIS countries and the Baltic States are connected with lower registration of unemployed persons at a PES; the proportion of benefit recipients in total unemployment would thus be even lower than in the CSEE countries. The replacement rates related to the average national wage reached a maximum of one-third in 1998, making it unlikely that unemployment benefits per se would discourage benefit recipients from taking up a job, were one available.

---

[17] For a detailed discussion of labour market policy, its formulation, implementation and outcomes, see Nesporova (1999).

Nonetheless, the unemployment problems of older workers and workers with disabilities have often been resolved by offering early retirement, pre-retirement benefits or disability pensions, as noted earlier. While workers themselves usually welcome this solution, it is expensive and burdens state budgets. In addition, a number of discouraged jobseekers, particularly those lower skilled, lower paid and often with health problems, have opted for living on social welfare, usually combined with some extra income from subsistence farming and informal casual activities. Policy-makers and social policy experts have debated this issue frequently in the recent past, preferring to cut social benefits and push such workers back into the labour market. Here the problem is the lack of low-skilled regular jobs available and the very low wages offered, which do not compensate for the additional costs of job take-up (such as transport and clothing).[18] Cuts in social welfare would lead to further deprivation of low-skilled or disadvantaged groups and often would not force them into employment.

## Active LMP

In all transition countries, PES systems were established in the initial phase of economic and social reforms, and play a significant role in mediating jobs to job-seekers seeking re-employment assistance. In 1998 the share of registered jobseekers placed in new jobs with the assistance of PES ranged from 19 per cent in Ukraine to 63 per cent in the Russian Federation. PES officials estimate that on average about one-third of job placements were through public labour offices; this figure may not appear high but it is of consequence for less competitive groups of workers.[19]

Apart from job mediation, these countries designed and implemented a number of active labour market programmes, ranging from vocational training, job creation measures and subsidized employment to mobility promotion. At the outset, due to the lack of experience and skills of PES staff, problems arose with the formulation, targeting and application of these programmes, so that re-employment rates after their completion were initially low; however, these have improved over time. But the biggest problem – the financial situation – remains. National employment funds are already stretched to pay benefit entitlements and to combat high unemployment: what is left to spend on active LMP is very modest. There are also important cross-country differences in the funding of active LMP, which reveal a weak correlation between the level of expenditure and the size of national labour market problems (for more detailed analysis and discussion, see Chapter 6, table 6.2).

Besides income support in unemployment, early retirement and disability pensions, the level of social benefits and assistance may also have an important effect on the decision to withdraw from or return to the labour market. For example, in the

---

[18] The frequently proposed solution to reduce the minimum wage in countries such as Poland or Slovenia, in order to stimulate creation of new jobs for low-skilled workers, will thus probably not improve the situation.

[19] This information is based on interviews with PES officials in the transition countries. The OECD database for OECD countries gives a figure of the share of PES placements in all new hirings ranging from 1 to 38 per cent.

CIS and non Central European countries the level of social welfare is low in general, whereas studies on the Czech Republic and Estonia show that for a family with low-wage earners, the difference between income from employment and income from social transfers is negligible, and that the latter is higher when job take-up costs are considered.[20] These two countries have recently increased the minimum wage to make employment a more attractive alternative to living on social welfare.

## 2.2.6  The impact of income policy

The transition countries inherited low levels of wages (excluding non-monetary benefits) and rather low wage differentials. This was due to their fairly rigid central pay systems, which set wages according to the industry and type of work rather than the skill requirements, employee performance or the economic performance of the enterprise. Economic reforms gradually replaced centralized wage tariff systems with wage determination based on collective bargaining in the enterprise sector, while maintaining a universal tariff system in the budget-funded sector. Most countries have also introduced the minimum wage as a basis for the wage tariff system in both the budget-funded and the enterprise sectors, but often also for calculating minimum social benefits. In many countries, however, the minimum wage has fallen well below the subsistence minimum, thus losing its social and economic function.

In line with price liberalization, governments also introduced economic stabilization programmes in which the key role was attributed to a tax-based income policy, controlling wage increases above a specified level through a punitive tax. The aim of this policy, imposed in most countries on state-owned enterprises, was to link wage increases more with enterprise performance and to lower a price–wage inflation spiral. The direct consequence of this tax-based income policy was a sharp fall in real (consumer) wages in 1993, equal to around 80 per cent of their 1989 level in the Czech Republic, 71 per cent in Poland, 66 per cent in the Russian Federation and down to 38 per cent in Ukraine. Wage regulation contributed to the disconnection of wages and productivity. The more profitable enterprises were not allowed to increase wages above the agreed maximum. Meanwhile, poorly performing enterprises increased wages to the maximum, under pressure from their workers, often at the cost of postponing investments, defaulting on existing loans or increasing borrowing. Small differences in wages between profitable and non-profitable enterprises did not stimulate the desired reallocation of labour from the latter to the former, and thus significantly contributed towards delaying enterprise restructuring: redundant workers remained in large enterprises while more productive enterprises could not attract workers by significantly higher wages.

Moreover, monopolistic enterprises, mainly in the extraction industries, metallurgy and energy, converted their profits (artificially inflated by price increases) into higher and faster-growing wages than those in other industries, without changing

---

[20] See, for example, Večerník (2001) and Arro, Eamets et al. (2001).

technologically or raising productivity. In addition, particularly in the CIS countries, huge wage arrears emerged as a consequence of the collapse of market demand and the heavy taxation of enterprises. A credit squeeze, induced by restrictive monetary and fiscal policies, deprived enterprises of working capital, while cuts in government spending resulted in mounting wage arrears in both the enterprise and the budget-funded sectors. Wage regulation was moderated and finally abolished, leading to a more rapid recovery of real wages, although by 2000 only the Czech Republic had achieved real consumer wages exceeding their 1989 level.

## 2.2.7  The effect of collective bargaining

Over the course of the past decade the majority of transition countries moved towards a collective bargaining system at national and enterprise level. In contrast, industry-wide and regional collective bargaining is still much less developed or even missing in a number of transition countries. Tripartite consultation and negotiation at the national level has been preferred as it has directly involved the social partners in economic and social reforms, making them more cooperative in effecting difficult economic adjustments, and has thus facilitated the transition process. The established national tripartite bodies have dealt with the liberalization of wage policy, the level of wages and incomes, the regulation of working conditions and the protection of workers against the risk of redundancy and unemployment. At the enterprise level, less often at the industry level, collective bargaining between employers (represented by the management) and workers (usually represented by trade union organizations) should result in the conclusion of collective agreements.[21] The percentage of workers covered by collective agreements is fairly high in the public sector and in large private firms. Workers in medium-sized and small firms are rarely unionized.

Collective bargaining at the enterprise level usually concentrates on negotiations on wages and working conditions. Employment issues are of less importance and focus more on compensation in case of redundancy rather than on prevention of redundancies. Major exceptions are the coal mining and steel industries, where strong trade unions have opted for strike action, temporarily blocking mass dismissals in order to have them coincide with high severance payments. In the CSEE countries, EPL usually only stipulates that the enterprise trade union organization should be informed of redundancy intentions. In a number of CIS countries, trade unions are required to agree with lay-offs (which may, and did in the past, effectively prevent redundancies) and to compel enterprise managements to turn to alternative cost reduction measures, such as administrative leave or non-payment of wages. In Poland and Romania, for example, the power of trade unions has been translated into stronger protection of jobs in enterprises. In addition, privatization deals, particularly in Poland, included temporary bans on mass redundancies. The expiry of such privatization clauses after 1998 was one reason for the rapidly increasing unemployment in this country.

---

[21] For more on the progress and outcomes of collective bargaining in the transition countries, see Casale (1999).

## 2.3 CONCLUSIONS

The aim of this chapter has been to analyse labour market developments in transition countries after 1989. It endeavours to contribute to the debate on the reasons why unemployment in the countries under review has remained so high and is recently again on the increase, despite economic recovery and even solid growth rates finally achieved by all these countries. It has also sought to explain significant differences in unemployment levels among transition countries, rather weakly dependent on their economic performance.

The response to the first question can be found in the effort of enterprises to increase labour productivity and become competitive through the elimination of labour hoarding and the use of labour-intensive technologies, while cutting employment in the public sector for budget reasons. Informal employment also plays an important role in the persistently high unemployment rates.

Cross-country differences were explained by a combination of factors, ranging from different starting conditions and changes in the quantity and quality of the labour supply – through substantial variations in national monetary and fiscal policies, the methods of privatization of state-owned enterprises, policies encouraging FDI and new enterprise development, as well as legal and institutional reforms – to disparities in national industrial relations, income, labour market and social policies. The aim of this analysis was to point to the complexity of reasons for persistently high unemployment in the transition countries without making any attempt to quantify the impact of all the factors enumerated (which would be very difficult due to their interrelated character). The rest of the book will concentrate mainly on the role of employment protection legislation, labour market institutions, social dialogue and labour taxation, and will attempt to quantify their impact on labour market performance.

The appropriate national policy response should take into account a combination of country-specific factors affecting the supply and demand sides of the labour market that contribute to its poor employment performance, and address them accordingly, while putting the long-term goal of decent work for all at the centre of economic and social policy.

# CHANGING CHARACTERISTICS
# OF EMPLOYMENT

# 3

The transition process brought fundamental changes to the structure of employment, by sector and by branch, in line with a production response to changing market demand. Other general characteristics of employment, such as its composition by status, type of contract and length of working time, also saw profound modifications. If under the central planning system typical employment used to be dependent, full-time and performed under regular labour contract without limit of time, under the new system the need of enterprises to flexibly adjust their labour input and costs to changing market conditions gave rise to the emergence of atypical forms of employment and their looser regulation. This chapter will provide a deeper insight into these changes.[1]

The chapter first studies changes in the structure of employment by economic sector. Using the data available, it looks at the development of self-employment and analyses the labour market effects of inflows of FDI and the privatization of large state-owned enterprises. It also gives evidence on an upsurge of flexible forms of employment. It investigates general trends and cross-country differences in the application of temporary labour contracts, agency work, civil and other contracts not governed by the labour courts, part-time employment, multiple-job holding and informal employment. Conclusions summarize the evidence on the changing characteristics of employment in transition countries.

## 3.1    SECTORAL CHANGES IN EMPLOYMENT

The analysis starts with a review of the sectoral composition of employment and its links to the economic development of the transition countries at the beginning of their economic reforms in 1990. It continues by describing and explaining the different effects of the transition crisis and consequent economic development on the changes in employment distribution between the primary, secondary and tertiary sectors and

---

[1] In this and subsequent chapters, we shall deal only with those countries for which reliable data are available, referring to this group under the general term of "transition" or "Central and Eastern European (CEE)" countries.

within the latter two sectors, comparing the five Central European countries with other transition countries.

It is widely accepted by development economists that there is a significant correlation between the level of economic development measured by GDP per capita and the employment structure by economic sector. With growing GDP per capita the share of agriculture in employment is expected to decline and the share of industry to first increase and later shrink, all in favour of expanding services. In the World Bank ranking, former European and Central Asian centrally planned economies belong to the group of medium-income countries, although with important differences among them: the Central European and the Baltic countries are placed in the higher-medium and the other countries in the lower-medium income groups.

## 3.1.1 Sectoral composition of employment at the beginning of economic reforms

As table 3.1 illustrates, in 1990 a generally high proportion of agriculture in total employment was more or less in line with the region's medium economic level, as standard economic development theory would predict. In general, the ranking of countries by shares of agriculture was inversely related to their ranking by GDP per capita, although there were certain countries with remarkably high employment in agriculture, such as Poland in the group of Central European countries, or the Baltic States inside the Soviet Union. Poland was atypical because, unlike in the other centrally planned economies, the collectivization of Polish agriculture was stopped in the initial stages for political reasons, after which farmers were simply protected against competition. However, without access to finance or new machines, they lacked the motivation to improve their performance, and while protected from collapse they could not expand. Over-employment in agriculture thus went hand in hand with low labour productivity. In contrast, the position of the Baltic States within the Soviet Union was exceptional, despite less favourable climatic conditions and lower quality of land. Their farms were smaller but used more productive agricultural technologies and machines, achieving higher crops per hectare and lower losses during harvest and storing. Since the quality of their produce was also highly valued by Russian consumers, the Baltic farms had wide access to the vast Russian market.

In contrast with agriculture, in 1990 the share of industry was very high in most countries in relation to market economies at a similar economic level. The main difference was the strong accent put on heavy industry by political leaderships of these countries in line with the theorem of a primacy of "production of production means" over "production of consumer goods", generating a vicious circle of production for production's sake, with few goods produced for sale (see, for example, Komarek et al., 1990). Heavy industry was also essential for the immense military sector. As a consequence, industries producing consumer goods were relatively worse staffed, with considerably lower wages and lower labour productivity, mainly as a result of even more outdated technologies and equipment.

Table 3.1   Employment structure by sector, selected transition countries, 1990
and 1999 (percentages)

| Country | 1990 | | | 1999 | | |
|---|---|---|---|---|---|---|
| | Agriculture | Industry | Services | Agriculture | Industry | Services |
| Azerbaijan | 30.9 | 22.9 | 46.2 | 42.3 | 11.7 | 46.0 |
| Belarus | 21.6 | 38.5 | 39.9 | 21.2 | 34.9 | 43.9 |
| Bulgaria | 18.5 | 44.2 | 37.3 | 26.2[1] | 30.6[1] | 43.2[1] |
| Croatia | 14.8[2] | 41.8[2] | 43.4[2] | 16.6 | 30.6 | 52.8 |
| Czech Republic | 12.3 | 45.5 | 42.2 | 5.3 | 40.9 | 53.8 |
| Estonia | 19.4 | 37.5 | 43.1 | 8.8 | 32.2 | 59.0 |
| Hungary | 18.2 | 36.8 | 45.0 | 6.9 | 34.5 | 58.6 |
| Kazakhstan | 22.3 | 31.5 | 46.2 | 22.0 | 18.3 | 59.7 |
| Kyrgyzstan | 32.7 | 27.9 | 39.4 | 52.4 | 11.6 | 36.0 |
| Latvia | 17.1[2] | 38.4[2] | 44.5[2] | 15.3 | 26.1 | 58.6 |
| Lithuania | 18.4[2] | 42.6[2] | 39.0[2] | 20.2 | 26.9 | 52.9 |
| Moldova | 33.8 | 29.0 | 37.2 | 48.9 | 13.6 | 37.5 |
| Poland | 25.2 | 37.0 | 37.8 | 19.1[1] | 32.1[1] | 48.8[1] |
| Romania | 29.1 | 43.5 | 27.4 | 41.8 | 27.6 | 30.6 |
| Russian Federation | 13.9 | 40.1 | 46.0 | 13.9 | 29.3 | 56.8 |
| Slovakia | 13.7[2] | 45.5[2] | 40.8[2] | 7.4 | 38.5 | 54.1 |
| Slovenia | 9.4[2] | 46.6[2] | 44.0[2] | 8.5 | 38.8 | 52.7 |
| Tajikistan | 44.7[3] | 23.1[3] | 32.2[3] | 46.1[4] | 17.4[4] | 36.5[4] |
| Turkmenistan | 42.1 | 20.7 | 37.2 | .. | .. | .. |
| Ukraine | 20.0 | 39.8 | 40.2 | 22.8 | 25.9 | 51.3 |
| Uzbekistan | 39.3 | 24.1 | 36.6 | 39.4[1] | 19.2[1] | 41.4[1] |

Notes: [1] 1998. [2] 1989. [3] 1991. [4] 1997. .. not available.

Sources: Census data for 1990; labour force surveys for 1999.

As a result, services contributed much less to total employment in these economies than in other, non-transition, medium-income countries. The difference was most striking in the case of services for production as well as of distribution (trade, transport and communication), household and personal services, while social services, in particular education and health care, were relatively well represented. Perhaps surprisingly, the share of public administration employment was low, relative to similarly developed market economies. Common understanding was that under central planning the administrative apparatus was immense, but this was actually not true when compared with the size of public administration in industrialized countries.

However, it should be taken into account that many services were provided internally, within enterprises. They would often have their own transportation units, catering services, shops for workers, clinics and sanatoria, recreation centres, nurseries and kindergartens, housing for employees, and so on. As the basic statistical unit was the enterprise, in most countries, these internal services were counted as part of its main activity. The shares of industry, construction and agriculture thus appeared higher, while that of services was underestimated, compared with their actual proportions. The difference was substantial. In Czechoslovakia, a detailed statistical analysis of the 1988 employment structure by industry revealed that of the 48 per cent share of industry and construction in total employment as much as 6 percentage points were actually services (and should therefore be imputed to the tertiary sector), while only the remaining 42 per cent were genuine industrial and construction activities (Nesporova, 1993).

## 3.1.2 Structural changes over the 1990s

The transition crisis hit manufacturing initially for several reasons. A sharp fall in personal incomes coincided with the opening up of domestic markets to competition from cheap imports of consumer goods from South-East Asia and imports of higher-quality products from developed countries, suppressing demand for domestic consumer products. The collapse of the common market of the former Eastern bloc, followed within a short time by the break-up of the Soviet Union, resulted in a loss of external markets and distortion of existing production links among enterprises. Enterprises producing consumer goods were the first to feel the effects of deep recession. A severe decline in their demand for investment, as well as a withdrawal of subsidies from the state budget and an abrupt slump of state orders, soon pulled the rest of the manufacturing sector into recession, with a strong impact on overall economic development.

The search for new markets was much more successful for enterprises of the Visegrad countries (the Czech and the Slovak Republics, Hungary and Poland), Slovenia and Estonia, soon followed by Latvian and Lithuanian firms. These countries had stronger links with Western enterprises, many of which bought their shares and made further investments, establishing joint ventures or starting direct cooperation with them. Proximity to the EU markets, secure property rights and later also the start of the EU accession negotiations significantly aided in this move towards the West. Industrial recovery was crucial for economic recovery in general. This development contrasted with that in South-East Europe, where economic uncertainties connected with the Balkan wars and backlashes in economic reforms discouraged potential foreign investors, while heavily under-invested domestic enterprises were unable to upgrade production and therefore could only partially succeed in the export market. In the CIS countries the most competitive enterprises had until recently been concentrated in extraction and primary processing of natural resources, often in joint ventures with foreign capital. Devaluation of the national currencies after the financial crisis in Russia in August 1998 increased the competitiveness of domestic products over imported goods and contributed to a major revival of manufacturing not only in the Russian Federation but also in other CIS countries relying on exports to Russia.

While all the transition countries recorded a fall in the share of the secondary sector in total employment, a strong correlation could be found between the extent of job losses and job gains in industry and overall economic performance. Those countries in which employment losses in industry were more limited, i.e. in Central Europe, were those which had been able to halt the economic decline early and achieve positive GDP growth rates (see again tables 3.1 and 2.1 respectively). Large-scale structural changes within industry meant that massive job destruction from the period of transition crisis was counterbalanced to a large extent by job creation in expanding segments of manufacturing. Similar developments have also taken place in the construction industry in these countries. Big construction firms, which before 1990 had been engaged in large infrastructural projects or in building industrial premises or settlements of large prefabricated blocks of flats, shrank considerably or even disappeared in the transition period. This gap in the market has been filled by mushrooming small construction firms concentrating on construction, renovation and maintenance of housing and business premises. Hence, the resulting effect on employment has been less pronounced in these countries.

A share of agriculture in total employment sharply decreasing to well below 10 per cent can be seen as indirect evidence of positive structural changes, indicating that a substantial proportion of workers from former agricultural cooperatives or state farms were able to find jobs in other sectors of the economy. Other agricultural workers, especially those with little education, ended up in long-term unemployment or withdrew from the formal labour market (see, for example, Boeri, 2000). The only exception has remained Poland; it has managed to cut employment in agriculture by some 6 percentage points, but its very high proportion of agriculture in total employment – more than double the average of the other Central European countries – clearly shows that major agricultural reform is still ahead. The persisting larger share of the secondary sector in total employment, combined with its internal restructuring, is characteristic of the Central European countries, and it has been the decisive factor for early economic recovery and relative sustainability of economic growth.

In those countries that so far have been less economically successful in closing the gap between pre-transition GDP and its current level, the degree of de-industrialization has been considerably more profound: in the non Central European countries, industry lost more than 10 percentage points in its employment share in the first decade of economic transformation. Structural changes were of a more passive character, as massive job destruction was combined with little new job creation in industry. The sharp decline hit both manufacturing and construction because of low demand on the domestic market, while exports remained largely limited to raw materials.

Agriculture, on the other hand, maintained or even increased its contribution to total employment in this second group of transition countries, once it had absorbed a large number of those workers made redundant from industrial enterprises. Jobs created in agriculture are usually characterized by low productivity; family farms are poorly mechanized and the remaining agricultural cooperatives do not have enough finance to maintain their machinery. For many people, subsistence farming on their own plots of land has become an important source of income (although often this type of activity is performed in addition to primary employment, unemployment or formal economic inactivity and as such is usually not covered by labour statistics). In these countries, the steeper the drop in GDP, the larger the increase in the proportion of agriculture in total employment. This group of countries includes not only all the CIS countries but also some other European transition economies, among them even four EU accession candidates – Latvia, Lithuania, Bulgaria and Romania. While the first two States have recently achieved considerable progress in economic development and are already successfully catching up with the other Central European transition countries, the latter two still have further to go to put their economies on a fast and sustainable economic growth track.

These structural changes in the primary and secondary sectors brought consequences for the tertiary sector. The contribution of services grew fast in the majority of the transition countries although the absolute number of workers in services has increased significantly only in some countries (the Czech Republic, Lithuania, Poland, Romania, Slovakia, the Russian Federation or Ukraine, for instance). In other countries, particularly those having experienced a substantial decline in economic activity and total employment over the 1990s, the rise was more moderate (such as Croatia, Estonia and Slovenia), and in some (such as Bulgaria, Hungary and Latvia) employment in services actually declined. One important reason for an upswing of the tertiary sector was evidently a higher demand from consumers and enterprises – more extensive in Central Europe and the Baltic States, while usually more limited in other transition countries. Another source of this increase (and the simultaneous decline of industry, less so of agriculture) has been the externalization of services in the course of enterprise restructuring, in Central Europe in particular. While a larger part of services formerly provided by enterprises was shifted under the responsibility of municipalities or became independent, private or cooperative economic units, some of them unfortunately disappeared, such as childcare facilities or in-house training.

A certain part of the tertiary sector has expanded, as in agriculture, through increased self-employment in response to a shortage of dependent, decent jobs in other sectors of the economy. In fact, some of these jobs are informal, as their holders hide earnings for tax reasons, so the true proportion of services in total employment is likely to be even higher. New jobs in services are thus created on both sides of the decent work spectrum (see ILO, 2002). Those in the financial sector, business services or public administration, all of them having accelerated in the 1990s, require high skills and are among the best-paid jobs in the national economy. In contrast, many new jobs in distribution, personal and household services are of low quality in terms of stability, security, remuneration and working conditions.

If in 1990 the service sector contributed between 25 and 46 per cent to total employment in the transition countries, nine years later its contribution had grown to a level of 30 to 60 per cent, meaning that not only the average level but also cross-country differences had considerably increased. The coincidence of pull and push factors behind this enlargement of the tertiary sector, as well as the effect of declining participation rates in the formal economy, have resulted in a weaker correlation between economic development and the share of services in employment. Hence not only leading reformers (with the exception of Poland) exceeded the level of a 50 per cent share of the tertiary sector in employment, but also countries like Kazakhstan, the Russian Federation and Ukraine; this contrasts with the mere 30.5 per cent achieved by Romania or 43.2 per cent in Bulgaria.

Intensive restructuring has been taking place inside the tertiary sector as well. The explosion of small firms at the beginning of economic transformation was made up of new shops, restaurants, hotels and family guesthouses, travel agencies, transport firms and similar small-scale economic activities. However, with the arrival of large international retail companies, restaurant and hotel chains or transport enterprises able to operate with minimum trade margins and profit rates, suppressing market prices while benefiting from low labour costs and massive sales worldwide, many of these firms have been wiped out. This has been reflected in an initial acceleration of certain distribution and personal services and their later stagnation or even recent decline. Services related to production have recorded particularly rapid development over the transition period and some hold significant potential. This is true of research and development, despite its temporary slump in the first decade of economic transition due to lack of funds from both enterprises and the State. Adult education, social and health care services are also expected to expand in connection with labour market changes and an ageing population. Personal services will increase in line with rising personal incomes, and to a certain extent public administration and the police can be expected to grow in the future.

## 3.2 "PRIVATIZATION" OF EMPLOYMENT

### 3.2.1 Increase in self-employment

Under the political system of "real socialism", the role of private ownership in production was almost exclusively limited to self-employment: family farming in agriculture and small-scale activities in handicraft, art and some services. Moreover, for ideological reasons even self-employment had a disadvantaged status in comparison with the two alternatives of wage employment in state-owned enterprises and the budget-funded sector or collective employment in cooperatives. In fact, collective employment had gained the features of wage employment and over time the difference between them almost disappeared. Constraints on self-employment were considerable. Often the self-employed could not freely decide from whom to buy inputs and to whom to sell their outputs and for what price, they had little or no access to bank loans with which to expand production and usually could not hire any employees outside the family. Nevertheless, there were substantial differences among the countries as to the share of self-employment: in 1989 the figure was 8.5 per cent in Hungary, 26.9 per cent in Romania and 25.7 per cent in Poland, compared with 1 per cent in former Czechoslovakia and below 1 per cent in the former Soviet Union, according to national statistics.

Legal and economic reforms launched after political changes formally equalized all types of ownership, liberalized prices and trade, and started privatization of enterprises. So-called "small" privatization of shops, hotels, restaurants or individual production units was completed rather quickly in the majority of the transition countries, leading to an expansion of self-employment and private wage employment. It was often combined with the return of nationalized property to the former owners or their heirs, who used the acquired premises and equipment for their own businesses, rented them out or sold them to new entrepreneurs. Many new small firms also appeared as a result of formalization of certain informal activities from the pre-transition period or as a response to newly emerging market opportunities. A number of new private enterprises were offshoots of the restructuring of large enterprises that preceded or resulted from their privatization when ancillary production and services were externalized with the aim of increasing productivity both in the original enterprise and in the new unit.

Because of the fairly limited access to finance through the banks and the devaluation of individuals' savings by high inflation, self-employment grew mainly in labour-intensive activities, such as personal and household services, retail trade, catering and accommodation, handicrafts, the professions (for example, lawyers and doctors), transport and construction. Many such firms have been on the edge of formality for tax reasons: part of their activity is formal in order to benefit from tax-based cost deductions, while another, often much larger part remains informal and therefore not taxed at all. Nevertheless, the unexpected depth of the transition crisis and changes in market demand, along with a lack of experience and entrepreneurial skills, a shortage of capital, and administrative obstacles, have resulted in the failure of many new small businesses.

In contrast with these factors promoting self-employment and private wage employment, there was also high unemployment and low labour demand and a sharp decline in real incomes after 1989. As already described, those unable to find work or unwilling to accept a low-quality, poorly paid job often had no other means of earning a living but independently. A large number of self-employed workers are concentrated in subsistence farming on small private plots of land, in handicrafts and personal services. Activities of this kind are characterized by a low technological level, low capital intensity and low labour productivity so that their chances of surviving the pressures of competition and expanding are quite limited.

As family farming in Poland and Romania prior to political changes was at the same low productivity level, experts expected that a combination of new market opportunities and harsher competition in the agricultural market would lead to the selection of more competitive farmers and their expansion, while less competitive farmers would leave for non-agricultural jobs. However, in Poland this happened only to a limited extent because non-agricultural labour demand remained very weak. In Romania, the number of small private farmers has actually even increased because of land reform and massive lay-offs in industry, as a number of new landowners who had returned to their previously nationalized land were pushed into farming. This type of low-productivity work is, however, unstable in the longer run. When labour demand recovers, many such self-employed persons will try to return to dependent employment, otherwise they may withdraw from the formal labour market to inactivity and complement their social transfer income with casual informal activity.

There is one category of independent worker that is actually in wage employment, although this employment relationship is disguised. In order to save on contributions to social funds, as well as on costs of employment termination, employers – particularly in construction and services but also in manufacturing – push workers to become formally self-employed and offer them contracts for specific tasks/work (these "civil contracts" are discussed further in section 3.3.3). Sometimes both sides agree to share the saved taxes through higher remuneration for workers. However, even if workers can benefit from this arrangement in the short run, it will usually not cover them in the case of a work accident or occupational disease. When they are ill they receive no sickness allowance unless they are privately insured and they may risk losing their job, while forgoing employer pension contributions results in a lower old-age pension.

Considering the range of factors affecting the development of self-employment and their varying significance by country, there are substantial differences among the transition countries both in self-employment trends in the 1990s and in the actual share of self-employment in total employment, as reflected in table 3.2.

Despite changes in the gathering of labour statistics in the early 1990s and certain methodological discrepancies in the measurement of the share of self-employment in total employment before then, in general the data reveal a rapid growth of self-employment in the initial years of economic transition.[2] However, after this initial period of tapping new market opportunities, the development of self-employment has become more stable: still slowly growing in some countries (Bulgaria, the Czech Republic, Romania, Slovakia) but mostly stagnating or even declining (Croatia, Lithuania, Poland, the Russian Federation and Slovenia).

The explanation for this stabilization in self-employment levels appears to be connected on the one hand with a seemingly saturated demand for services at the current income level, but on the other hand also with a recent decrease in subsistence farming due to a certain recovery in non-agricultural labour demand. In addition, a large number of new small businesses are being pushed out of the market by the recent expansion of multinational chains of supermarkets, hotels, restaurants and enterprise catering providers, travel agencies and other service providers, as well as the entry of foreign-owned firms in manufacturing, and some of these small businesses are unable to survive by switching activity. Moreover, in some countries the national social protection system does not cover the self-employed: they are not eligible for unemployment insurance and cannot get disability benefits or social assistance unless they give up their business licence.

---

[2] The 1989 self-employment figures cited on p.37 are derived from establishment census data, while the data in table 3.2 come from labour force surveys. This explains the decline between 1989 and 1993 for Romania from a 26.0 per cent share of self-employment in total employment to 22.1 per cent, when an increase in the share of agriculture in total employment in this country, mostly attributable to subsistence farming, would imply the opposite.

Table 3.2    Self-employment as a share of total employment, selected transition
economies, 1993 and 2000 (percentages)

| Country | 1993 | | | 2000 | | |
|---|---|---|---|---|---|---|
| | Men | Women | Total | Men | Women | Total |
| Bulgaria | 12.9 | 9.2 | 11.2 | 18.3 | 10.6 | 14.7 |
| Croatia | 25.1[1] | 15.4[1] | 20.7[1] | 23.3[2] | 14.4[2] | 19.2[2] |
| Czech Republic | 15.8 | 9.4 | 12.8 | 18.8 | 9.0 | 14.5 |
| Estonia | 10.4 | 6.2 | 8.4 | 9.7 | 6.4 | 8.1 |
| Hungary | 17.4 | 11.3 | 14.6 | 18.7 | 9.6 | 14.6 |
| Latvia | 12.4[3] | 6.9[3] | 9.8[3] | 12.5 | 8.4 | 10.5 |
| Lithuania | 21.5[4] | 14.6[4] | 18.3[4] | 19.2 | 12.7 | 15.9 |
| Macedonia | 74.0[5] | 68.5[5] | 71.8[5] | .. | .. | .. |
| Poland | 32.2 | 29.9 | 31.2 | 25.9 | 18.4 | 22.5 |
| Romania | 24.4 | 19.4 | 22.1 | 32.6 | 17.4 | 25.4 |
| Russian Federation | 10.1[6] | 5.6[6] | 8.0[6] | 8.4 | 6.2 | 7.4 |
| Slovakia | 9.0 | 3.5 | 6.6 | 10.9 | 4.1 | 7.8 |
| Slovenia | 16.0 | 7.6 | 12.2 | 15.3 | 6.5 | 11.2 |
| Ukraine | .. | .. | .. | 8.3[2] | 9.0[2] | 8.6[2] |

Notes: [1] 1996. [2] 1999. [3] 1995. [4] 1997. [5] 1991. [6] 1994.  .. = not available.

Sources: Labour force surveys, authors' calculations.

Apart from the outstanding case of Macedonia, the share of self-employment in total employment has not exceeded one-third in the transition countries. Poland and Romania, but also Croatia, Lithuania and to some extent Slovenia, have the highest proportions of self-employment by a considerable margin. The explanation lies in the large numbers of family farms in these countries; in the case of Croatia and Slovenia it is also a legacy of the economic system in the former Yugoslavia, which permitted small private enterprises.[3]

For the EU accession countries the share of self-employment averages between 10 and 15 per cent, as in the majority of the EU Member States (with the exception of the southern countries), although there are surprisingly low levels in Estonia and Slovakia. In general it seems that, because of the legacies of the past, the current economic situation and the level of incomes, the proportion of self-employment has stabilized in this group for the time being.

At the other end of the scale with regard to self-employment are the former Soviet countries, partly because of the lack of entrepreneurial tradition. The main obstacle to the expansion of small businesses and other self-employed activities in the CIS countries (but also in many other transition countries) seems to be restrictive

---

[3] Some evidence suggests that differences among countries could become smaller if only non-agricultural self-employment were considered. However, the lack of data does not permit such a comparison.

administrative regulations which burden the life of small entrepreneurs. These bureaucratic difficulties range from an excessive number of certificates required for starting up a new firm; numerous regulations for running firms, with no exceptions for small ones; frequently changing legislation; high and complicated taxes plus frequently changing tax reporting; and pressures from local administration and state inspectors. These often exorbitant requirements can have a number of negative consequences: many potential entrepreneurs are deterred from starting their own business activity or give it up when any problems appear; discouraged small firms slip into informality and self-employed workers prefer to run their business as a second activity for tax purposes only, with no aspiration to expand and eventually create jobs for others. The administrative system is a major reason why a large part of subsistence activity remains hidden in the informal economy.

## 3.2.2 Employment effects of privatization of large enterprises and inflow of FDI

The greater part of privatization of employment in the transition countries came about through the denationalization of large state-owned enterprises. This took different forms and moved at different speeds in the various transition countries, with related implications for employment. Usually the countries combined several methods of privatization for large enterprises but they differed in the priority put on one or another technique. Countries such as Estonia and Hungary relied primarily on the direct sale of large and medium-sized companies to foreign investors, which was relatively transparent, generated considerable revenue for their state budgets and usually brought new investment capital and higher productivity. Foreign owners tended to quickly restructure the enterprise, cut off inefficient parts and lay off redundant workers. Inside buyouts by employees and managers were the second (but much less used) method of privatization and concerned only smaller and less important firms.

The Czech Republic, Lithuania and Slovakia (the last only in the first round of privatization) opted for mass privatization through distribution of vouchers to the population. While this approach was seen as very rapid and fair, it produced an extreme dispersion of share ownership with little control over enterprise management. In order to buy out the shares managed by investment funds (where small private shareholders placed their shares for management) or the remaining shares owned by the State, managements took credits from the banks for these purchases. They also turned to the banks for investment credit. However, enterprise profits were too low to allow proper loan servicing and most bank credits became non-performing, bringing the enterprises – many with viable production programmes – to financial collapse. In such a situation, managers often opted for rent-seeking and transfer of assets to their own firms, thereby depriving enterprises of scarce financial resources and accelerating their collapse. In order to maintain social peace for keeping their positions, enterprise managements tolerated labour hoarding for a significant period so that employment trends seemed quite favourable. The situation changed sharply when banks refused to continue providing credits to the enterprise, and the enterprise was unable to service the debt and went bankrupt (or was sold before bankruptcy). Direct sales to solvent, usually foreign investors have originally been the second method of privatization, but recently accelerated both in cases of collapsing enterprises from voucher privatization and privatization of remaining enterprises.

The CIS countries, in particular the Russian Federation and Ukraine, preferred subsidized management–employee buyouts of firms as their main method of mass privatization. This route to privatization was also very fast. But it generated little revenue for the State and no new investment capital for the enterprise, and led to corporate governance no more efficient than its Soviet counterpart. Compared with privatizations in the Czech Republic, Lithuania and Slovakia, the only difference was the greater influence of employees on hiring and firing within the enterprise. This resulted in a much higher level of labour hoarding and employment than in enterprises with similar economic performance in other countries. Enterprise managements engaged in asset-stripping and the exclusion of other owners (primarily workers), while foreign investors were not interested in injecting capital into enterprises with non-transparent ownership.

Conversely, Bulgaria, Poland, Romania and Slovenia were slow privatizers of their large state enterprises. Slovenia and to a large extent Poland succeeded in commercializing and restructuring these enterprises and putting them under hard budget constraints, with subsequent direct sales of many enterprises to private investors (in Poland these investors were usually foreign, and recently this has also been the case in Slovenia). Bulgaria and Romania continued to subsidize their state enterprises, although Bulgaria had to stop this practice with the introduction of the currency board in 1998. The efforts of Slovenia and Poland led to the substantial amelioration of enterprise corporate governance, resulting in improvements in enterprise performance but at the cost of massive job destruction and reductions in overstaffing.

The transition countries vary not only in the extent of involvement of foreign capital in large-scale privatization but also in the establishment of entirely new enterprises through FDI. To date, Poland has received the highest amount of FDI in the region (on a cash basis, US$28.5 billion over 1990–2000).[4] However, in terms of a cumulative inflow of FDI per capita over the same period, the first places are held by the Czech Republic (US$2,200) and Hungary (US$2,100), followed by Estonia (US$1,680), Croatia (US$1,055), Latvia, Slovenia, Slovakia, Poland and other countries. While until 1997 only Hungary could boast a significant inflow of FDI per capita, since 1998 the primary recipients have become the Czech Republic and Poland. This move is connected with the recent accelerated privatization of state-owned infrastructure companies and state banks, but also with the establishment of large new enterprises.

The effect of FDI on job creation and job preservation has been both positive and negative. The initial direct effect is considered as positive, although in privatized enterprises it is usually associated with cuts in labour hoarding, profound restructuring and destruction of redundant jobs. However, the entry of FDI also leads to the exclusion

---

[4] This and the following figures are taken from or calculated on the basis of UNECE, 2001, table B17, p. 177.

of less profitable domestic competitors and the replacement of many domestic supplies with imports from the company's usual foreign sources. Very often, foreign-owned companies may thus create a sort of isolated island with few linkages to the domestic economy. Hence, the overall effect on employment very much depends on the purpose of FDI inflow into the country. It may be export-oriented, with a high import content, and based on exploitation of low labour costs, or it may be more driven by the good quality of domestic infrastructure, competitiveness of domestic suppliers and skills of the workforce. In the first scenario, the final employment impact is limited, very insecure in the longer run and contributes little to the country's economic development. The second scenario is more promising from the point of view of development benefits for the country, but can have either positive or negative effects on employment, depending on whether the purpose of the investment is to cooperate with domestic producers or to rule them out of the market.

The level of FDI that a country attracts depends on several factors: its political and economic stability; progress in EU accession negotiations; proximity to the parent company abroad; incentives for foreign investors; market prospects; and the expected profitability of the investment project, including access to cheap and skilled labour. Obviously, the Central European accession countries are much better off than the rest of the region and they benefit considerably from FDI in terms of new job creation or preservation of existing jobs.

Regardless of whether the "privatization" of employment has occurred as a result of small- or large-scale privatization, the establishment of new small firms or the entry of FDI, its speed has been impressive. By 1995 the share of employment in the private sector had exceeded the share of public employment, and by 1998 private employment contributed almost 90 per cent to total employment in Estonia, close to 80 per cent in Poland, 70 per cent in the Czech Republic and over 60 per cent in the Russian Federation and Bulgaria.

## 3.3   INCREASINGLY FLEXIBLE FORMS OF EMPLOYMENT

While under the previous regime flexible forms of employment were rather exceptional and limited only to certain categories of workers (for example, managers, academics and a few other white-collar professions, plus seasonal workers in agriculture and food processing), since 1989 they have become more frequent and available to more categories of workers, both white-collar and blue-collar. Under flexible forms we understand here labour contracts with limited duration (fixed-term and short-term contracts), agency work (work for a fixed, short period arranged by a staffing agency), part-time employment, multiple-job holding and work agreements between two parties for certain tasks or activities. The last two forms in particular are closely interrelated with informal employment.

The use of flexible forms of work has expanded with the need of employers to adjust their production profile and costs to market conditions, and to do so relatively smoothly. A good deal of anecdotal evidence from the transition countries now shows that when internal redeployment of redundant workers is not possible or convenient for the employer, due to skill mismatches, economic difficulties or a lack of suitable jobs, the response is not to upgrade the skills of employees or to reskill them; instead, the adjustment of labour input is often made through lay-offs in periods of economic downswing and hirings of persons with required skills during economic upswings. As national employment protection legislation is stricter in the case of workers with contracts without limit of time, requiring certain administrative procedures (advance notice, consultation with the trade union organization, special protection for socially vulnerable groups, and so forth) and severance pay, employers prefer to turn to more flexible forms of employment relations. These enable faster adjustment of the number of employees in accordance with the actual market and financial situation of the enterprise, while simultaneously reducing costs of employment termination.[5] The facility of the use of flexible contracts instead of permanent ones varies by country, although in general the expansion of temporary contracts has been enabled by amendments in EPL since the start of the reform process, considerably moderating workers' employment protection.

## 3.3.1   Temporary labour contracts

Table 3.3 shows the shares of temporary contracts among all employment contracts in selected transition countries for the years 1993 and 2000.

With the exception of Estonia, the general trend in all the transition countries has been an increase in the proportion of temporary contracts in employment contracts in the 1990s. The most marked change has occurred in the Czech Republic and Slovenia: these countries also have the highest shares of temporary contracts among the Central European countries, with 8.1 per cent and 12.9 per cent respectively in 2000. In contrast, the proportions of temporary contracts in Estonia, Romania and the Russian Federation did not exceed 3 per cent in 2000, and Estonia even experienced a slight decline in this indicator between 1993 and 2000. Despite this upward trend, comparisons with the EU countries show that the incidence of temporary contracts is still much lower in the transition countries. In the majority of the EU countries the tendency is also towards a higher use of time-limited contracts, facilitated by the deregulation of employment relations. By the end of the 1990s their share exceeded 10 per cent in the EU countries, with particularly high levels in Finland, Portugal and Spain (see, for example, European Commission, 2001).

As for the incidence of time-limited contracts by sex, there is no systematic difference between men and women. In Slovakia, Slovenia and the Czech Republic more women hold temporary contracts than men, and in the latter two countries, moreover, their increase has also been higher for women. However, in a number of other transition countries, their use is either similar for both sexes (Romania) or the situation is the reverse – higher for men than for women (Estonia, Hungary, Latvia, Lithuania and Poland).

---

[5] For more on this issue and a discussion of its advantages and disadvantages for employers, workers and society, see Chapter 5, section 5.2.

Table 3.3   Temporary employment as share of wage employment, by sex, selected transition countries, 1993 and 2000 (percentages)

| Country | 1993 | | | 2000 | | |
|---|---|---|---|---|---|---|
| | Total | Men | Women | Total | Men | Women |
| Czech Republic | 5.1 | 4.8 | 5.5 | 8.1 | 7.0 | 9.4 |
| Estonia | 4.5 | 4.8 | 4.2 | 2.3 | 3.1 | 1.4 |
| Hungary | 6.6[1] | 7.0[1] | 6.3[1] | 6.9 | 7.3 | 6.4 |
| Latvia | .. | .. | .. | 6.7 | 8.8 | 4.6 |
| Lithuania | .. | .. | .. | 3.8 | 5.1 | 2.7 |
| Poland | 5.5 | 6.0 | 4.9 | 5.8 | 6.6 | 4.8 |
| Romania | .. | .. | .. | 2.9 | 3.0 | 2.9 |
| Russian Fed. | .. | .. | .. | 1.5 | .. | .. |
| Slovakia | .. | .. | .. | 4.0 | 3.8 | 4.3 |
| Slovenia | 8.9 | 8.7 | 9.0 | 12.9 | 12.4 | 13.5 |

Notes: [1] 1997. .. not available.

Source: National labour force surveys (1993 data for the Czech Republic, Estonia, Poland and Slovenia and the 1997 data for Hungary directly from national sources; 2000 data for all countries from Eurostat, 2001)

Although no information is available on the distribution of temporary contracts by age, anecdotal evidence, indirectly supported also by the short average job tenure among young people below 25 (see Chapter 4, table 4.7) indicates that young people are overrepresented among temporary contract holders and probably face considerable problems in the transition from temporary to permanent contracts.

The reason for the relatively low application of temporary contracts until now may be certain legislation rigidities and the opposition of trade unions, but also a significant decline in the length and costs of employment termination for employers. All these issues are discussed in the following chapters. Obviously, the trade unions oppose the weakening of EPL, in particular the expansion of flexible forms of employment, calling for limitation of the number of consecutive contracts. Therefore the extent of these forms in a given country is also an indicator of the trade unions' power there. There may also be different practice for small firms, for whom permanent contracts may be unacceptable due to their volatile position in the market, and any limits on temporary contracts are only related to larger companies (in Poland, for example, limits apply to firms with more than 20 employees). Some countries still (for example, Bulgaria) or have until recently (for example, the Russian Federation) limited the use of fixed-term contracts to certain situations or groups of workers (such as enterprise managers and academics) or they specify groups to whom such contracts cannot be offered (for example, to school-leavers in the Czech Republic), as will be illustrated in Chapter 5.

## 3.3.2 Staffing agency work

No data on staffing agency work (such as Manpower) are provided by national statistics, but anecdotal evidence shows very limited use of agency work to date in any transition country for groups of people other than students (of secondary schools and universities). Agency work by students has traditionally been organized by student agencies, and more recently also by other specialized agencies. New subsidiaries of foreign staffing agencies or similar domestic agencies are still rather rare, as employers are not accustomed to this type of services. For the temporary replacement of absent workers they have tended to rely on regularly hired workers. The exceptional character of temporary agency work is also the reason why thus far no transition country has regulated it through specific legislation.

## 3.3.3 Civil and other non-employment contracts

"Civil contracts", concluded between two parties for a certain task or activity within an agreed period of time and regulated by civil rather than labour law, existed before 1989 but their incidence was limited to casual or seasonal activities unconnected to the main employment or other economic status of the worker. Since 1989 these contracts have increasingly been used as a substitute for regular employment contracts, as employers find them administratively and financially convenient.[6] Unlike regular employment contracts, employers are not obliged to provide these workers with safety equipment, in principle they are not responsible for any eventual occupational disease or accident in the workplace, and when civil contracts are concluded employers do not need to cover social contributions. Termination of such agreements is very simple, without any obligation for either of the two parties, while early termination, before the agreed date, entails little penalty if any. Because of the limited duration of such contracts, workers are not entitled to any seniority pay based on the length of service (regardless of often repeated contracts with the same person which mean that the actual job tenure may be quite long) so that the total remuneration for these workers is low, as are the total labour costs for employers.

Those working on civil contracts are usually statistically counted as the self-employed if this is their main activity or according to their primary employment status if this is their second activity, but the evidence is often imprecise. In order to stop the misuse of such contracts and increase revenues of social funds, some countries (for instance, Poland in 1996) have restricted the application of civil contracts to those activities of a character other than that of a regular employment relationship or clearly stipulated conditions under which civil contracts can be agreed. This has indeed led to a certain reduction in their use (see, for example, Kwiatkowski, Socha and Sztanderska, 2001, or Beleva and Tzanov, 2001).

---

[6] An example may be helpful. A construction company concludes civil contracts with several bricklayers on building a house instead of hiring them as regular employees. The bricklayers are formally self-employed, responsible for paying contributions to health, pension and social welfare funds, although their job description is the same as that of regular employees for whom the employer has to cover a significant part of these contributions.

Any hard statistical data concerning the spread of civil contracts in the economy are very rare. In Bulgaria the labour force survey has recently included questions concerning the type of contract worked under, whether employment or civil. The data reveal that in 2000 the incidence of civil contracts was slightly over 7 per cent (7.3 per cent in March 2000 and 7.1 per cent in June 2000) for the whole economy. However, there was a striking difference between the public and the private sectors as to the use of civil contracts: while the public sector applied this type of contract only in slightly more than 1 per cent of cases, private employers used them in more than 14 per cent of their total wage employment. In the Russian Federation, the share of civil contracts was 0.7 per cent in 1999.

As to other labour work arrangements outside of the remit of employment law, in 2000 on average 7.5 per cent of employees worked under such conditions in Bulgaria: 1.5 per cent of workers held non-specified contracts and around 6 per cent of workers had no contract at all. While the share of contracts or other arrangements for work not regulated by employment law accounted for only 2 per cent in the public sector in Bulgaria, in the private sector this proportion equalled 29 per cent. The percentage of this type of contract among employees was much more limited in other transition countries: 0.5 per cent in the Czech Republic (2000), 2.8 per cent in Estonia (1998) and 3.7 per cent in the Russian Federation (1999), according to national labour force surveys.

## 3.3.4  Part-time employment

Table 3.4 presents data on part-time employment in selected transition countries. This cross-country comparison reveals several findings, which distinguish these countries from the industrialized ones.

First, with the exception of Latvia, Poland and Romania, only a small proportion of workers work part time. Workers are not very interested in shortening their working hours and earnings because the low level of wages means that any wage reduction has an impact on the household budget. Employers also prefer full-time employment, claiming that part-time contracts do not usually bring sufficient cost reduction to counterbalance the negative effect of the unavailability of part-time employees to their colleagues and clients during regular working hours, while job sharing in fact poses additional costs.

Second, there are large differences across the range, which are probably to be attributed to the extent of underemployment in the country, although unfortunately few data are available to confirm this hypothesis. The only available data for the Czech Republic and Estonia indicate that in the former country the share of involuntary part-time employment[7] was around one quarter of total part-time employment, while in the latter this proportion was already around or slightly over one-half during the 1990s. Ostensibly, the sole reason for part-time employment in

---

[7] Involuntary part-time employment means that job holders have had to accept part-time employment because they could not find full-time employment.

Table 3.4    Part-time employment as share of total employment, by sex, selected transition countries, 1993 and 2000 (percentages)

| Country | 1993 | | | 2000 | | |
|---|---|---|---|---|---|---|
| | Total | Men | Women | Total | Men | Women |
| Bulgaria | 3.0[1] | .. | .. | 0.6 | 0.8 | 0.5 |
| Czech Republic | 6.3 | 3.0 | 10.3 | 5.3 | 2.2 | 9.2 |
| Estonia | 5.0 | 3.6 | 6.7 | 6.7 | 4.2 | 9.3 |
| Hungary | 3.2[2] | 2.1[2] | 4.4[2] | 3.2 | 1.8 | 5.0 |
| Latvia | 13.1 | 12.2[2] | 13.9[2] | 10.7 | 9.5 | 12.1 |
| Lithuania | .. | .. | .. | 8.6 | 7.6 | 9.6 |
| Poland | 10.7 | 8.9 | 12.9 | 10.6 | 8.4 | 13.2 |
| Romania | 14.7[2] | 12.2[2] | 17.6[2] | 16.4 | 14.3 | 18.6 |
| Russian Federation | 5.2 | .. | .. | 5.6[3] | .. | .. |
| Slovakia | 2.3[4] | 1.0[4] | 3.7[4] | 1.7 | 0.9 | 2.8 |
| Slovenia | 5.2 | 4.4 | 6.1 | 6.1 | 7.7 | 4.7 |

Notes: [1] 1994. [2] 1997. [3] 1999. [4] 1998. .. = not available.

Source: National labour force surveys; data for 2000 taken from Eurostat, 2001.

the Russian Federation is temporary or permanent lack of work (see Tchetvernina et al., 2001). Higher part-time employment may therefore indicate higher involuntary underemployment in the country.

Indeed, faced with financial problems many enterprises in transition countries turn to shorter working hours of all or certain categories of workers to bridge this difficult period. This reduction is often reflected in labour force surveys as part-time employment, regardless of whether the affected workers hold part-time contracts or are forced to work shorter hours without any change in their (full-time) labour contract. This practice of short-time work or even administrative leave is a well-known feature of the CIS countries but it is not uncommon in other transition countries. The CIS countries collect and publish separate data on the number of workers involved in short-time work and administrative leave, based on establishment surveys, while labour force surveys in other transition countries probably mix short-time with part-time workers.[8]

The Russian Federation provides a good illustration of the use of temporary reductions in work hours. The annual share of persons forced to take administrative leave in the Russian Federation reached the highest level in 1996 with 16 per cent of average payroll numbers in large and medium-sized enterprises, falling to 11 per cent in 1998 and 8 per cent in 1999. Of these workers, 48 per cent did not receive any compensation. The average length of administrative leave per worker was almost

---

[8] Limitations of the data from these two sources are discussed in some detail in Chapter 4.

stable: 318 hours in 1996 and 311 in 1999. The share of workers on the payroll put on a short-time work regime at the initiative of enterprise management moved from 7.2 per cent in 1996 to 10.1 per cent in 1998 and 6.5 per cent in 1999. The number of hours lost per worker due to a short-time regime was 332 in 1997 and 188 in 1998 (see Tchetvernina et al., 2001).

The third finding to come from the data presented in table 3.4 is that there was no general trend in part-time employment over the 1990s. Some countries have experienced a certain increase in the share of part-time employment in total employment (most notably Estonia and Romania), while others have recorded a decline (Czech Republic and Latvia) or almost no change.

Fourth, while women workers are overrepresented among part-time workers in the majority of the selected transition countries, as is the case in industrialized countries, in Bulgaria and Slovenia there are more males than females working part time. A more frequent incidence of part-time work among women is connected with their primary responsibility for childcare and care of the elderly, still rarely done by men, and this arrangement enables them to combine employment with family responsibilities. Moreover, in some transition countries women can combine part-time employment with maternity/parental leave without losing entitlement to allowances, and this is quite often utilized.

Apart from women, young people below the age of 25 and older workers aged over 50 are also overrepresented among part-time jobholders. In Estonia, for example, while the proportion of part-time workers in total employment in 1997 was 7.1 per cent, among workers between the ages of 15 and 24 it was 8 per cent and for those aged over 50 it was 11 per cent. Young people usually combine part-time work with education; however, in some countries and notably in Slovenia, they also take part-time employment because of the difficulty they face in finding full-time jobs. In contrast, older workers generally work part time because of health problems.

## 3.3.5 Multiple-job holding

Multiple-job holding is another form of flexible work arrangement, where workers hold a second, usually part-time, activity besides their main job. Figures provided by national labour force surveys usually refer to legally contracted jobs and suggest significant differences between the transition countries, as illustrated in table 3.5.

The data indicate that the extent of multiple-job holding negatively correlates with the economic level of the country, that is to say that the more economically developed countries tend to have lower shares of workers engaged in two or more jobs, and vice versa. This phenomenon seems to apply more to a "survival strategy" for poorer households trying to gain an additional source of income, which is obviously much more important in less economically advanced countries. For firms, this type of employment also seems to be advantageous, as second-job holders are usually weakly protected by legislation against employment termination.

Multiple-job holding is closely interrelated with informal employment. With the exception of unregistered foreign migrant workers, the extent of informal

Table 3.5   Multiple-job holding as share of total employment, selected transition
countries (percentages)

| Country | Reference year | Multiple-job holding as share of total employment |
|---------|----------------|----------------------------------------------------|
| Armenia | 1999 | 16.2 |
| Croatia | 1998 | 18.8 |
| Czech Republic | 1999 | 2.8 |
| Estonia | 1999 | 7.2 |
| Kyrgyzstan | 1997 | 4.1 |
| Poland | 1998 | 10.0 |
| Russian Federation | 1998 | 12.8 |
| Ukraine | 1999 | 27.5 |

Source: National labour force surveys for all the countries except for the Russian Federation, for which Longitudinal Monitoring Survey data were used. With the exception of the Czech Republic and Estonia, the data are taken from the European Bank for Reconstruction and Development, 2000, table 5.3.

employment performed as a primary activity is rather limited in the transition countries, as it often prohibits access of such informal workers to social security and health care insurance. Therefore the vast majority of informal workers perform this activity as a second job besides their main formal employment, registered unemployment or inactivity, combined with some sort of welfare transfer. This is particularly characteristic of Central Europe, but less so of some CSEE countries or the CIS. As already mentioned in Chapter 2, in Poland the share of persons performing informal work in 1998 accounted for 4.8 per cent of the population aged 15 and over, while 5.5 per cent of employed persons had an informal activity as their second job. Among the registered unemployed, 14.6 per cent revealed informal activity and 2.4 per cent of informal workers were among those formally economically inactive.

With regard to unregistered employment, the Polish LES figures on multiple-job holding given above seem to seriously underestimate its scale. A survey undertaken for the research project Social Stratification in Eastern Europe after 1989 provides much higher figures for secondary activities: 5 per cent for the Czech Republic, 9 per cent for Slovakia, 17 per cent for Poland and 27 per cent for Hungary in 1993 (Večerník, 2001, p. 9). Although these figures were collected in 1993 when the four countries had just emerged from the transition crisis, they still indicate higher actual shares of multiple-job holders among all workers. Indeed, another survey on Economic Expectations and Attitudes, conducted by the Czech Academy of Sciences in 1994 and including a wider scope of activities, both formal and informal, revealed even higher figures for the Czech Republic. In 1994, a total of 35 per cent of the economically active population declared a supplementary activity: 27 per cent active in a second job, 28 per cent self-employed and the remainder earned in "some other way". A repeated survey in 1998 under the same project reported a decline in the share of secondary activities to 28 per cent, which was still ten times higher than the "official" figures of the labour force survey.

In the Russian Federation two recent surveys undertaken by the All-Russia Centre of Public Opinion (VTsIOM) show that between 11 per cent and 17 per cent of the working population had second jobs in 1997–98. Between 33 and 44 per cent of second jobs were performed for the same employer, 19–23 per cent were service-oriented small-scale activities (repair, maintenance, dressmaking, and so on), 9–19 per cent were done in other enterprises and 4–5 per cent were in trade (Tchetvernina, 1999). A broadly shared view among labour economists is that many more persons have second jobs in the informal economy, usually in subsistence farming activities producing for the extended family and regularly or occasionally also for the market. According to one estimate, 10 per cent of the employed population had formal or informal second jobs performed regularly and another 30 per cent occasionally (Clarke, 1998). Russian sources themselves vary substantially on this issue. The Russian Tax Inspectorate estimated the share of the adult Russian population having second jobs as around 35–40 per cent (Simagin, 1998), while a Presidential representative addressing the State Duma on this topic in 1998 put the estimate at 90 per cent (Varshavskaya and Donova, 1998).

## 3.4   CONCLUSIONS

Economic and social reforms and the effect of globalization on the national economies of the transition countries have resulted in vast modifications in the structure and characteristics of employment. First of all, they have contributed to significant changes in the structure of employment by economic sector. While in the longer run all the countries will undoubtedly follow the general development trends of employment flowing from agriculture to industry and from both these sectors to services as the economy progresses, the depth of the transition crisis in less economically developed countries has temporarily reverted these trends in part. On the one hand, employment in industry declined everywhere, although more in countries experiencing deeper recession. On the other hand, the latter group of transition countries has experienced stagnation or even an increase in employment in agriculture, which has had to absorb a part of redundant workers from industry. The share of services in employment has increased, but partly as a similar buffer for unemployment as agriculture.

The share of workers employed in the private sector as opposed to those active in the public sector has also increased dramatically. Several factors contributed to this privatization of employment: domestic business start-ups, including all types of self-employment; privatization of existing enterprises; and FDI into existing or newly established enterprises. This chapter has explained the diverse employment effects of different privatization methods used in the transition countries. "Private" employment in enterprises privatized by voucher method or insider buyouts was little different from "public" employment in not-yet-privatized state-owned enterprises in terms of the productivity requirements on workers, unless the enterprises were put under hard budget constraints. This development contrasted with that of other countries using direct sales of enterprises or their parts to solvent investors, domestic or more usually foreign, as their principal method of privatization has usually led to cuts in labour hoarding, a significant increase in labour productivity and in a number of cases new private employment creation.

The effect of "greenfield" FDI has been positive in creating new jobs but rather often also negative in ruling domestic competitors out of the market or replacing domestic suppliers with foreign ones and thus causing significant job destruction in the affected firms.

The number of self-employed workers (both registered and not) has sharply increased in all the transition countries in the initial period of economic transformation as a consequence of both push and pull factors. However, their share in total employment has now more or less stabilized everywhere owing to a combination of persistent administrative barriers for small business development; limited new opportunities for small businesses facing saturated consumer demand for the quality of products and services offered at such a low level of income and profit; and the low quality of many non-wage jobs. As a result, with increasing demand for wage employees and offers of higher wages, many self-employed workers are returning to wage employment.

The pressure on enterprises to adjust their production patterns and costs to changes in market demand has contributed to the increasing shares of flexible forms of employment. However, there are some distinct features in this overall trend in the transition countries. Part-time contracts are not widespread in the region, in particular because of the low level of wages. While in general the use of temporary labour contracts has significantly increased, this is particularly true of civil contracts not regulated by employment law, although hard data on the latter are rarely available. Many employers endeavour to save on non-wage costs by replacing regular employment contracts with non-employment ones, despite their ban under such circumstances in a number of transition countries. However, the major form of flexible employment after 1989 seems to be holding second or multiple jobs, both formal and informal, which are performed besides main formal employment, registered unemployment or formal inactivity.

# LABOUR MARKET DYNAMICS IN THE 1990s: A COMPARATIVE ANALYSIS

# 4

The aim of this chapter is to examine labour market dynamics in selected transition countries and their relation to economic and employment developments over the 1990s. How has the transition process accelerated labour adjustment in firms? Has it led to more unstable and insecure employment than was the case under the former system of central planning?

The chapter starts with a description of the trend in labour turnover since 1990 in selected transition countries. Through the analysis of job turnover we then examine the speed of restructuring taking place in these countries. After addressing this issue, the chapter goes on to examine job stability on the basis of job tenure data and reasons for separation in order to determine the extent to which the past model of secure long-term jobs has disappeared. Because of the limited availability of reliable data on this topic, as we shall discuss below, this chapter restricts its scope to a discussion of Bulgaria, the Czech Republic, Estonia, Hungary, Lithuania, Poland, the Russian Federation, Slovenia and Ukraine.

## 4.1    LABOUR TURNOVER IN THE 1990s

### 4.1.1  Data and sources

Labour mobility and intensity of labour reallocation are best reflected in labour market flow data. Under the command system, in principle all types of enterprises and organizations were obliged to deliver statistical data on such elements as production, investment and labour, including data on recruitments and separations. Consequently, national statistical offices published aggregate data on accessions and separations for the state and cooperative sectors (excluding agricultural cooperatives), and some countries also produced data divided by origin of accession and cause of separation.

With the transition to a market system and the corresponding methodological changes, there are now two sources of employment flow data: those based on establishment surveys and those originating in labour force surveys. The former source of information has become less comprehensive and reliable. First, it covers only enterprises employing over a certain number of workers, and this number not only differs by country but may also differ by sector. This is a considerable limitation as the share of small and micro firms and self-employment in total employment has escalated during economic transition, as described in the previous chapter. The second problem with establishment surveys is that the quality of data delivered is often poor. Enterprises may wish to hide or bias certain facts for tax or other reasons, and statistical bodies have limited ways of checking the data. Privatization and enterprise restructuring, as well as enterprise mergers and acquisitions, may also cause considerable data bias, as both newly established or privatized entities and old firms may formally recruit or lay off workers who in fact do not change their jobs. Labour turnover based on establishment surveys is calculated as a sum of recruitments and separations by individual establishments over a given year, divided by their initial or average employment levels for that year.

Labour force surveys are a new statistical instrument for transition countries, introduced gradually during the 1990s in an increasing number, although not all, of these countries. Thus, large discrepancies exist among countries in the time periods for which data are available, in the frequency of surveys, and in the range of information covered and made available to the public. Although microeconomic data on changes in labour market status are regularly collected, it is only recently that some national statistical offices have begun to estimate selected aggregate flow data regularly and provide them to Eurostat. In addition to this information worked on by Eurostat, some researchers have used rough data from labour force surveys to make their own calculations of labour market flows.[1] Labour turnover based on labour force surveys is a sum of the aggregate accession and separation rates. The accession rate is calculated as a sum of aggregate flows from unemployment to employment, from inactivity to employment and from one employment to another, divided by initial or average employment in a given year.[2] The separation rate is a sum of aggregate flows from employment to unemployment, from employment to inactivity and from one employment to another, divided by initial or average employment in a given year.

### 4.1.2 A comparison of labour turnover in selected transition countries

Available data from both sources of information – establishment survey data for Bulgaria, the Russian Federation, Slovenia and Ukraine; labour force survey data for

---

[1] For example, Haltiwanger and Vodopivec (1998); Arro, Eamets et al. (2001); Kwiatkowski, Socha and Sztanderska (2001); and Večerník (2001), who provided data calculated by them for the Czech Republic, Estonia and Poland. For Hungary and Slovenia the calculations have been made and kindly provided to us by departments responsible for labour force surveys in the National Statistical Offices.

[2] As in the case of establishment surveys, an imprecise definition of job-to-job changes may be an important source of data distortions, especially in comparative studies. For this reason we could not use all the available data, in particular when there was a strikingly wide difference between the results of establishment surveys and labour force surveys, as in the case of Slovenia.

the Czech Republic and Estonia; and, for Poland, both – reveal a substantial increase in labour turnover for our sample of transition countries after 1989, as can be seen in table 4.1. This reflects not only a reduction of the formerly widespread practice of labour hoarding as enterprises cut their labour costs, but also the growing incidence of voluntary quits by people deciding to start their own business or to join a newly established firm. This initial phase of intensive labour reallocation occurred in the first couple of years following the introduction of economic reforms: in 1990–92 in the CSEE countries and about two years later in the countries of the former Soviet Union. During that phase separation rates markedly exceeded hiring rates, indicating widespread downsizing in large and medium-sized enterprises. It should also be noted that downsizing was often connected with the splitting of large enterprises into two or more new firms, and with the outsourcing of production support services and services for workers.

Labour turnover subsequently declined and stabilized, though all countries have since continued to experience periodic surges in labour turnover (as did Bulgaria in 1997 and 1999 and the Czech Republic after 1998, for example). These reflect further structural changes connected with economic imbalances and remedial policy packages. The Russian financial crisis of 1998 caused a considerable economic shock, with particularly adverse consequences for countries such as Estonia and Ukraine on account of their substantial trade with the Russian Federation. This too increased labour turnover.[3] The Kosovo crisis had a negative impact on Bulgaria and contributed to accelerating separations from larger enterprises.

There are significant inter-country differences, both in rates of labour turnover and in the relationship between accession and separation rates. An outstanding example is Poland, where high labour turnover throughout the decade suggests intensive structural adjustment at enterprise level.[4] While Polish enterprises significantly reduced their workforce until 1993, hirings have outnumbered separations since 1994, reflecting net job creation in the economy, not only in large and medium-sized enterprises but also in small ones. This differentiates Poland from all the other transition countries in the sample. However, the data series does not extend beyond 1998 and therefore fails to capture the recent reversal of this positive trend since 1999, as reflected in Poland's rising unemployment.

Surprisingly, of all the countries reviewed, the Russian Federation experienced the highest labour mobility (at a relatively stable level) over the 1990s. This also could indicate extensive structural changes; but a significant decline in GDP argues

---

[3] For the Czech Republic and Estonia, the data for 1999 are unfortunately not available, but a sharp increase in their unemployment rates offers indirect evidence of higher labour turnover.

[4] The two labour turnover series show substantial differences, however: according to ES data, labour turnover declined significantly after 1991 with a new upswing in 1995–96 and again in 1998; the LFS data indicate a rapid increase after 1992, well above 50 per cent, and a similarly steep decline after 1996. This reflects the significant difference between the development of large and medium-sized enterprises and that of newly created, smaller firms. Before 1994, labour market changes were mainly determined by large enterprises, whereas after that date the strong economic recovery offered market opportunities for new, small enterprises. Since 1998, the restructuring of large enterprises in coalmining and the steel industry has again dominated labour market dynamics, as measured by the enterprise survey.

Table 4.1   Labour turnover, accession and separation rates for selected transition countries in the 1990s (percentages)

| Country | Source | 1990 | 1991 | 1992 | 1993 | 1994 | 1995 | 1996 | 1997 | 1998 | 1999 |
|---|---|---|---|---|---|---|---|---|---|---|---|
| **Accession rates** | | | | | | | | | | | |
| Bulgaria | ES | 20.0 | 14.7 | 12.6 | 15.4 | 18.1 | 20.9 | 21.3 | 27.4 | 26.0 | 27.6 |
| Czech Republic | LFS | .. | .. | .. | 22.6 | 18.6 | 14.5 | 12.2 | 12.6 | 10.5 | .. |
| Estonia | LFS | 14.9 | 18.0 | 23.0 | 25.6 | 27.6 | 15.8 | 20.8 | 17.7 | 16.0 | .. |
| Poland | ES | 12.2 | 16.1 | 17.9 | 20.6 | 21.0 | 23.3 | 25.0 | 20.2 | 24.6 | .. |
| Poland | LFS | .. | .. | 16.4 | 22.8 | 28.5 | 25.6 | 28.5 | 21.9 | 21.2 | .. |
| Russian Federation | ES | .. | .. | 22.9 | 21.1 | 20.8 | 22.6 | 18.9 | 19.9 | 21.0 | 24.2 |
| Slovenia | ES | 9.6 | 11.8 | 12.5 | 14.1 | 15.3 | 14.5 | 14.8 | 14.3 | 14.6 | 16.6 |
| Ukraine | ES | .. | .. | .. | .. | .. | 17.5 | 15.6 | 14.7 | 15.4 | 16.7 |
| **Separation rates** | | | | | | | | | | | |
| Bulgaria | ES | 28.9 | 36.2 | 31.1 | 29.6 | 25.8 | 22.5 | 24.8 | 31.9 | 29.8 | 39.9 |
| Czech Republic | LFS | .. | .. | .. | 22.0 | 17.5 | 15.8 | 12.6 | 12.2 | 11.8 | .. |
| Estonia | LFS | 15.9 | 20.4 | 31.4 | 30.0 | 27.7 | 16.2 | 22.1 | 18.5 | 19.0 | .. |
| Poland | ES | 23.0 | 26.8 | 22.4 | 21.0 | 20.7 | 21.9 | 22.3 | 16.9 | 22.8 | .. |
| Poland | LFS | .. | .. | 19.3 | 21.2 | 25.7 | 21.5 | 24.9 | 18.7 | 17.0 | .. |
| Russian Federation | ES | .. | .. | 26.9 | 25.1 | 27.4 | 25.7 | 23.9 | 24.5 | 24.9 | 24.5 |
| Slovenia | ES | 17.5 | 22.4 | 19.1 | 18.1 | 16.7 | 16.9 | 16.4 | 15.0 | 14.2 | 14.5 |
| Ukraine | ES | .. | .. | .. | .. | .. | 21.3 | 22.0 | 20.6 | 19.8 | 20.7 |
| **Labour turnover** | | | | | | | | | | | |
| Bulgaria | ES | 48.9 | 50.9 | 43.7 | 45.0 | 43.9 | 43.4 | 46.1 | 59.3 | 55.8 | 67.5 |
| Czech Republic | LFS | .. | .. | .. | 44.5 | 36.1 | 30.3 | 24.8 | 24.7 | 22.3 | .. |
| Estonia | LFS | 30.8 | 38.4 | 54.4 | 55.6 | 55.3 | 31.0 | 42.9 | 36.2 | 35.0 | .. |
| Poland | ES | 35.2 | 42.9 | 40.3 | 41.6 | 41.7 | 45.2 | 47.3 | 37.1 | 47.4 | .. |
| Poland | LFS | .. | .. | 35.7 | 44.1 | 54.2 | 47.1 | 53.4 | 40.1 | 38.2 | .. |
| Russian Federation | ES | .. | .. | 49.8 | 46.2 | 48.2 | 48.3 | 42.8 | 44.4 | 45.9 | 48.7 |
| Slovenia | ES | 27.1 | 34.2 | 31.6 | 32.2 | 32.0 | 31.4 | 31.2 | 29.3 | 28.8 | 31.1 |
| Ukraine | ES | .. | .. | .. | .. | .. | 38.8 | 37.6 | 35.3 | 35.2 | 37.4 |

Notes: ES = enterprise survey. LFS = labour force survey.   .. = not available.

Sources: National statistics. LFS data from Arro et al., 2001; Vecernik, 2001; and Kwiatkowski, Socha and Sztanderska, 2001.

against any massive restructuring for higher efficiency in the allocation of labour. In the case of the Russian Federation, large-scale labour reallocation is partly a legacy of the past, when workers moved between existing jobs in order mainly to improve their wages slightly and to gain access to enterprise-provided services. Large numbers of workers have been exposed to forced administrative leave and shortened working time, and many have not been paid wages for an extended period. As a result, they usually quit the enterprise voluntarily in order to find a financially more secure job (see Gimpelson and Lippoldt, 1997). But since new job creation has been very limited until recently, they mostly ended up in a similar type of job. Since 1999, more economically sound jobs have been created and positive structural changes seem to be taking hold. This is also reflected in an increase in the accession rate, which moved closer to the level of the separation rate and matched it in 1999.

Labour turnover in Ukraine has been much lower than in the Russian Federation, although both countries share the same problems of high underemployment and non-payment of wages, creating incentives for workers to move among existing jobs. The lower level of mobility in Ukraine is best explained by the country's much deeper economic recession, which has made workers more reluctant to leave their poorly paid jobs. The wide gap between hiring and separation rates, which still shows no sign of closing, points to a severe limitation of new job creation. On both indicators, Ukraine compares negatively with other transition countries – evidence of very slow redeployment of labour to more economically viable sectors, which has contributed to the country's negative economic growth since the start of the reform process.

Bulgaria witnessed very high rates of labour mobility in the first two years of reform, indicating massive job destruction in large and medium-sized enterprises which peaked in 1991. Between 1992 and 1996, labour turnover decreased, mainly as a result of a substantial decline in separation rates, while the hiring rate gradually recovered. However, the country's financial collapse in 1996 resulted in a steep upswing of labour mobility with a one-year lag. The Currency Board established in 1997 cut almost all subsidies to large state enterprises and forced the Government to accelerate their privatization. This led to their restructuring and large-scale downsizing, particularly in 1999. Simultaneously, the hiring rate increased substantially, pointing to the strengthening of structural changes, with a positive effect on economic growth.

In Estonia, the Government's very liberal approach to reform stimulated massive restructuring of enterprises and extensive reallocation of labour. Between 1992 and 1994, labour turnover reached the highest level recorded among all transition economies, with high rates of hiring and separations alike. Following this period of accelerated restructuring, the labour market gradually stabilized. However, with separations still exceeding recruitments, the overall effect of structural changes on employment has been negative for the whole transition decade.

Slovenia offers a somewhat different picture. Stimulated by economic reforms in the early 1990s, its labour turnover increased and then stabilized, albeit still at a fairly low level compared with the other countries. The first three or four years of transition were marked by a wide gap between separation and accession rates: enterprises had accumulated excess labour which they were forced to shed under the impact of economic reforms, while new hirings were limited. Between 1994 and 1997, both rates converged, though separations still outnumbered hirings. Since 1998, recruitments have accelerated and finally exceeded separations, with a positive impact on overall employment.

The Czech Republic recorded high labour turnover in the initial phase of transition. Unfortunately, the available data cover only the end of this phase. However, rapid changes in the sectoral structure of employment, together with declining participation rates and increasing unemployment, provide clear evidence of extensive labour reallocation in this period. Since 1993, labour turnover has declined considerably, indicating rapid stabilization of the labour market. Renewed structural changes in response to economic recession after 1997 are, unfortunately, not covered by the available data. It is also important to note that labour turnover data for the Czech Republic are not fully comparable with those available for other countries, as they underestimate job-to-job moves.[5] Moreover, unlike Poland, where calculations sum up quarterly flows, the data for the Czech Republic (and for Estonia) are annual and do not take into account multiple changes during the year. The data therefore underestimate aggregate labour market flows.

### 4.1.3 Labour turnover versus job turnover: A comparative analysis of the pace of restructuring

Labour turnover reflects the speed of labour reallocation in the economy. It results from the dynamics of job creation and job destruction, as well as from moves by employed persons among existing jobs and moves from unemployment or inactivity to employment and vice versa. In theory, structural changes relate only to the process of job creation and destruction, while labour turnover in excess of job turnover – sometimes called "labour churning" – points to labour mobility connected with other, non-structural reasons.

The purpose of the following analysis is to determine the extent of labour reallocation linked to structural changes by looking at the share of job turnover in labour turnover. It is also interesting to compare the ratio of job to labour turnover in the transition countries with that of the OECD countries, where it ranged from 25 to 40 per cent over the late 1980s and early 1990s (see OECD, 1994 and 1996).[6]

Job creation, job destruction and the resulting job turnover are usually calculated on the basis of enterprise surveys as the sum of changes in the number of jobs in individual enterprises, i.e. the sum of all employment gains from new or expanding enterprises and all employment losses from closed or downsized enterprises. Such data are not officially collected in any of the countries under review. However, a rough estimate of job turnover in a sample of transition countries can be derived from the enterprise databases maintained by chambers of commerce and industry or similar institutions, and from enterprise surveys undertaken by statistical offices.[7] Faggio and Konings (2000) and Gimpelson and Lippoldt (1997) provide such estimates for five

---

[5] For methodological reasons it was not possible to separate job-to-job moves from continuous employment for some 20 per cent of the persons covered by the LFS (see Vecernik, 2001).

[6] Boeri (1995) puts the ratio of job to labour turnover for the OECD countries at between one-third and half.

[7] Such surveys and databases cover only large and medium-sized enterprises and may not include newly established (particularly private) enterprises, nor do they consider employment losses in closed-down enterprises.

countries: Bulgaria, Estonia, Poland and Slovenia over the period 1994–97, and the Russian Federation in 1994–95, i.e. the period of relative economic stabilization and recovery that followed the initial, turbulent stage of transformation. The rates of job turnover and labour turnover are given in table 4.2.

Table 4.2 shows significant inter-country differences. Estonia, for example, is characterized by relatively high job turnover, accounting for almost 40 per cent of overall labour mobility in the period under review. This confirms that liberal economic reforms have accelerated structural adjustment of the Estonian economy, resulting in the highest economic dynamics achieved in the region. Slovenia, although often criticized for the slow restructuring of its large state-enterprise sector, actually boasts the second highest rate of job creation/destruction among the transition countries under review. Many experts took its low labour turnover for a symptom of slow economic transformation, but as we saw in our discussion of the privatization of state enterprises in Chapter 3, structural changes also explain this country's satisfactory economic performance in the 1990s.

In Bulgaria and the Russian Federation, by contrast, low job turnover is clear evidence of delayed restructuring of enterprises, resulting in poor economic performance for both countries. The wide gap between job turnover and labour turnover thus reflects the unduly high incidence of workers' moves among "old" jobs with low productivity and remuneration, rather than any positive reallocation of labour to new industries and enterprises. Rather surprisingly, Poland comes close to these two slow reformers in terms of both low job turnover and the latter's small contribution to labour mobility. The main reason seems to be that the enterprise survey used for calculating job turnover covered only large and medium-sized enterprises which, at the time, faced serious economic problems due to pending privatization and structural reforms. Robust economic growth was mainly driven by

Table 4.2   Comparison of labour turnover and job turnover for selected transition economies, 1994–97 (percentages)

| Country | Labour turnover | Job turnover | Ratio of job to labour turnover | Excess job reallocation rate[1] |
|---|---|---|---|---|
| Bulgaria | 48.2 | 8.1 | 16.8 | 4.8 |
| Estonia | 41.4 | 16.0 | 38.6 | 13.5 |
| Poland | 42.8 | 8.5 | 19.9 | 6.3 |
| Russian Federation[2] | 48.2 | 6.5 | 13.5 | .. |
| Slovenia | 31.0 | 9.5 | 30.6 | 8.5 |

Notes: [1] This is the difference between job turnover and the absolute value of the net employment growth rate. It can be used as an indicator of the extent of restructuring. [2] Only 1994–95.   .. = not available.

Sources: For labour turnover data, see table 4.1; job turnover data for Bulgaria, Estonia, Poland and Slovenia from Faggio and Konings, 2000, and for the Russian Federation, from Gimpelson and Lippoldt, 1997.

newly established enterprises, which attracted many workers from ailing state firms, but their contribution to job creation is not reflected in the available estimation of job turnover. That such is the case is confirmed by the difference between accession and separation rates taken from enterprise and labour force surveys, as presented earlier.

## 4.1.4 Labour turnover and the economic cycle

Labour turnover is of course significantly affected by economic fluctuations. In industrialized countries, it typically accelerates in periods of economic growth: enterprise start-ups and expansions create new jobs, attracting newcomers to the labour market and increasing hires of unemployed jobseekers. At the same time, though dismissals for economic reasons abate, the growing number of job opportunities encourages more people to change their jobs voluntarily. In economic downturns, by contrast, labour turnover declines: enterprises seek to cut costs by reducing new hires and by resorting to redundancies, yet the consequent sharp reduction of voluntary quits more than counterbalances the increase in dismissals. Largely for supply-side reasons, labour turnover thus tends to behave pro-cyclically (Boeri, 1995; ILO, 1996). In the transition economies, however, this pattern appears to be reversed, as shown in figure 4.1.

The correlation coefficients of labour turnover to both GDP and employment growth rates for the selected countries are presented in table 4.3. Yet there is always a time lag between a change in a country's economic performance and the translation of that change into decisions by enterprises to adjust their workforce and decisions by workers to change their jobs or stay put. The same correlations have therefore also been calculated with a time lag of one year. Cross-country comparisons are impaired by the fact that the labour turnover data series are rather short for some countries. The results therefore have to be interpreted with caution.

The correlation coefficients of labour turnover to GDP in table 4.3 (LT vs GDP) indicate a negative correlation for Ukraine, Estonia and the Russian Federation – albeit not very strong in the latter two cases – and a positive correlation for Poland. For the other countries, there seems to be no correlation between the two indicators. However, the time-lagged coefficients (LT vs GDP –1) show the correlation to be negative and generally stronger for almost all of the countries – the exceptions being Bulgaria and Poland (the latter calculated using establishment survey data).

Table 4.3 also presents the correlations of labour turnover with employment growth (LT vs E and LT vs E –1). As labour supply generally exceeded demand in all the countries of the sample after 1990, employment was mainly determined by demand for labour. Logically, one would thus expect a strong relationship between economic growth and employment and, therefore, the same type of correlation between employment and labour turnover as that between GDP and labour turnover. However, the situation is not necessarily that straightforward. Indeed, the translation of economic fluctuations into employment changes is always delayed because of labour market regulations (protecting workers against dismissal) and the significant costs of training, which induce employers to look for other solutions before they

Table 4.3    Correlations between GDP and employment dynamics (E) versus labour turnover (LT), selected transition countries

| Country | LT vs GDP | LT vs GDP (−1) | LT vs E | LT vs E (−1) |
|---|---|---|---|---|
| Bulgaria | 0.1977 | 0.0257 | −0.0757 | 0.3342 |
| Czech Republic | 0.0572 | −0.4832 | 0.0102 | −0.5652 |
| Estonia | −0.4616 | −0.7574 | −0.4926 | −0.7512 |
| Poland | 0.4927[1] | 0.2650[1] | 0.4023[1] | 0.2717[1] |
| Russian Federation | −0.3993 | −0.2789 | −0.2709 | 0.0684 |
| Slovenia | −0.0382 | −0.4673 | −0.3998 | −0.5107 |
| Ukraine | −0.7266 | −0.6367 | 0.6049 | 0.1322 |

Note: [1] Establishment survey data.

Sources: Authors' calculations based on data from table 4.1 (labour turnover) and UNECE, 2000 (GDP).

decide to recruit or dismiss workers. As described above, the link between economic growth and employment has been comparatively weak in a number of transition countries, because of extensive labour hoarding, technological changes, and labour market and social policies that tend to reduce labour supply.

In Estonia, the same strong negative correlations exist between employment and labour turnover, on the one hand, and between economic growth and labour turnover, on the other. The same goes for Poland, though the correlations are in this case positive. This pattern suggests a strong relationship between economic and employment developments in both countries. For Ukraine, by contrast, the correlations are respectively positive and negative, suggesting a rather peculiar link between GDP and employment developments. When a time lag is introduced, a strong negative correlation emerges between labour turnover and the employment rate in Estonia, Slovenia and the Czech Republic. That the same relationship occurs between GDP and labour turnover as well indicates a strong link between economic growth and employment developments in these three countries. For Poland and Ukraine, however, the correlations become insignificant.[8]

Overall, the calculations presented in table 4.3 invite the tentative conclusion that labour turnover tends to follow a countercyclical pattern in the transition countries, which indeed contrasts with the situation in the advanced industrialized countries. The explanation lies in the structural imbalances accumulated under the system of central planning because of the distortion of relative prices and poor economic performance of many investment projects. As a result, when these economies were suddenly opened up to global competition, industries with excessive capacity or non-competitive industries were hard hit, while underdeveloped services and competitive

---

[8] For possible explanations of these results by country, see Cazes and Nesporova (2001).

Figure 4.1  Labour turnover, GDP and employment growth in selected transition
countries, 1990–99

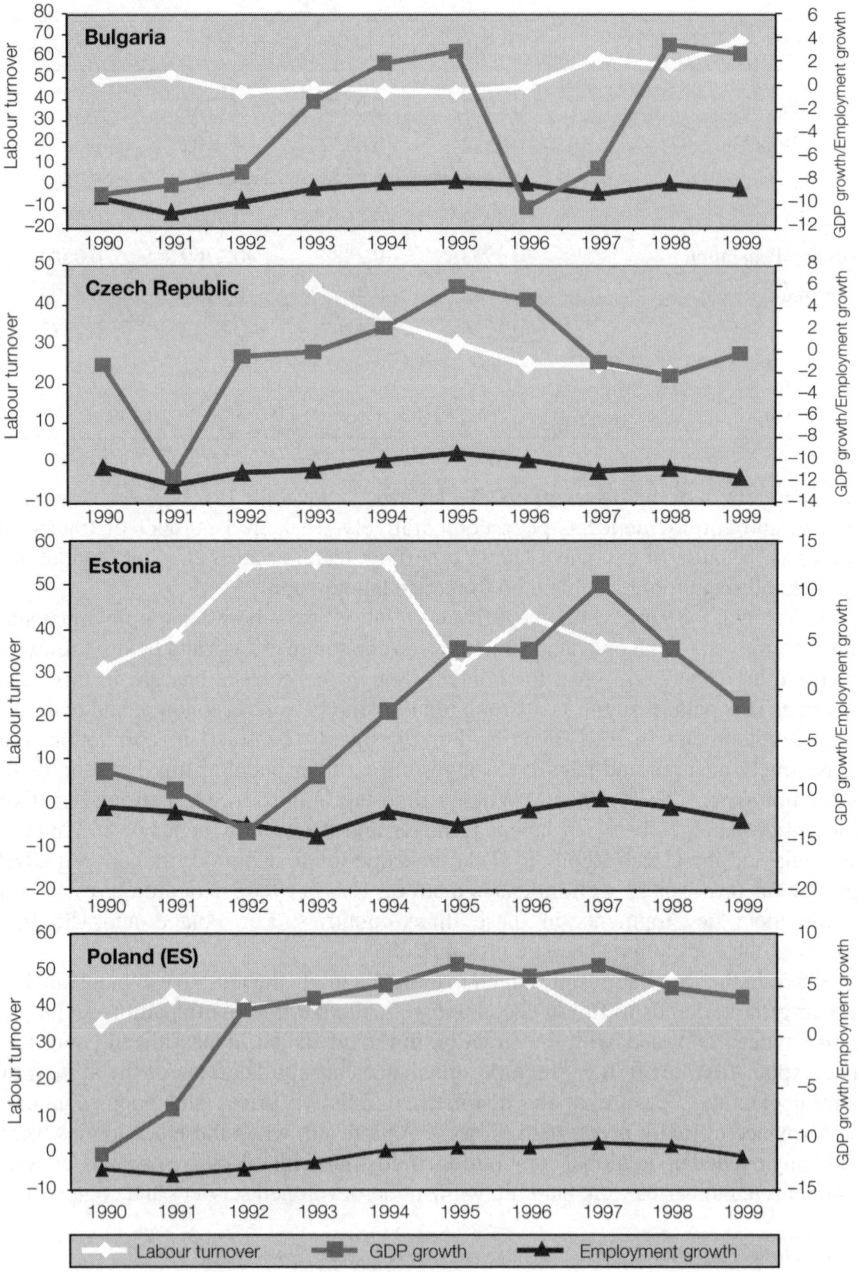

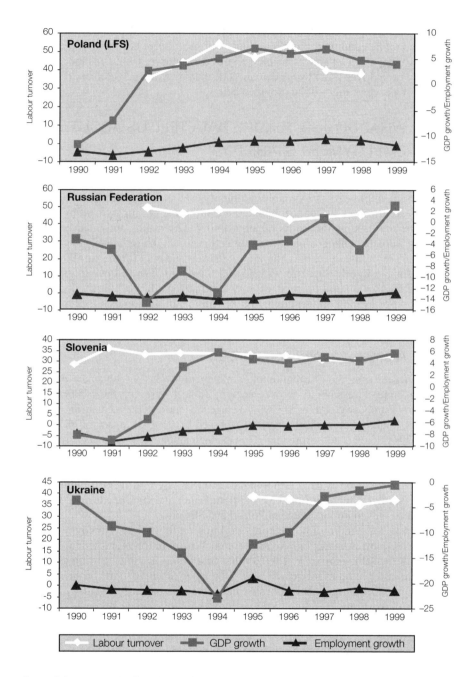

Sources: Labour turnover data from table 4.1; GDP and employment figures from UNECE, 2000.

manufacturing expanded. Outcomes have differed by country, depending inter alia on initial economic conditions and the adequacy of subsequent economic reforms. But unlike what typically happens in industrialized countries, labour reallocation has generally been driven more by the demand side than by workers' voluntary decisions. Further evidence of this will be provided below.

## 4.2   WHAT DO JOB-TENURE DATA TELL US ABOUT EMPLOYMENT STABILITY?

Job tenure – the length of time that currently employed individuals have spent with their present employer – is a variable commonly used in studies that focus on labour market stability. Average job tenure and the distribution of employment by class of job tenure are used as indicators of job stability. The results presented below are based on Eurostat data, complemented by national data. Unfortunately, data on job tenure are scarce, available only for a few countries and only for the past three years (except for the Czech Republic, Poland and Slovenia). The following assessment therefore focuses mainly on cross-country comparisons. It analyses the length and distribution of average job tenure across age groups by sex, industry, occupational group and qualification level.

### 4.2.1   A cross-country comparison

Average tenures and the distribution of employment by class of job tenure provide a general picture of job stability across countries. Table 4.4 presents these indicators for six Central European countries in 1999. Average job tenure in these countries was then 9.3 years, slightly below the 10.5 years averaged by the EU, Japan and the United States. This finding is not surprising, given the high labour turnover that characterizes the majority of transition economies. The two Baltic States have the lowest job tenure, with 6.9 years for Estonia and 7.6 years for Lithuania (close to the United States average of 6.6 years), followed by the Czech Republic and Hungary with average tenures below 10 years (similar to those of Denmark, the Netherlands and the United Kingdom). The longest average tenures are found in Poland and Slovenia.

Average job tenure is a function of hires (inflows into employment) and separations (outflows from employment), and of the duration of individual employment with the same employer. The fact that changes in hiring and firing affect the aggregate distribution of job tenure makes the latter sensitive to the business cycle. One might indeed assume that job tenure increases in boom periods (since a buoyant economy makes firms more inclined to offer stable jobs) and decreases in recession periods (as workers lose their jobs and general economic uncertainty induces firms to increase the flexibility of their workforce). Yet several factors affect the cyclical behaviour of job tenure: when employment growth recovers, more jobs are created and more people hired, which automatically reduces average tenure (because new recruits start with zero tenure). Moreover, voluntary quits also increase, because of

Table 4.4    Distribution of employment by job tenure, 1999, selected transition countries (percentages)

| Job tenure (% of total employment) | Czech Republica | Estonia | Hungary | Lithuania | Poland | Slovenia | Unweighted average | Standard deviation | Selected OECDb |
|---|---|---|---|---|---|---|---|---|---|
| < 6 months | 6.3 | 10.4 | 6.1 | .. | 5.1 | .. | 8.8 | 3.4 | 8.5 |
| 6 – 11 months | 8.3 | 8.0 | 6.5 | 12.8 | 5.4 | 12.0 | 7.1 | 1.3 | 7.8 |
| 1 – < 2 years | 18.4[1] | 6.7 | 11.3 | 9.2 | 10.4 | 5.1 | 8.6 | 2.6 | 8.8 |
| 2 – < 5 years | 15.3[2] | 31.1 | 20.0 | 29.0 | 14.0 | 18.2 | 22.5 | 7.3 | 15.0 |
| 5 – < 10 years | 26.2 | 23.9 | 25.3 | 24.8 | 20.8 | 16.5 | 22.9 | 3.6 | 19.0 |
| 10 – < 20 years | 12.3 | 10.8 | 17.9 | 14.5 | 22.3 | 23.6 | 16.9 | 5.3 | 21.9 |
| > 20 years | 13.2 | 9.1 | 13.0 | 9.6 | 22.0 | 24.6 | 15.2 | 6.5 | 19.0 |
| **Total** | **100.0** | **100.0** | **100.0** | **100.0** | **100.0** | **100.0** | **100.0** | **..** | **100.0** |
| Average tenure (years) | 8.2 | 6.9 | 8.8 | 7.6 | 11.9 | 12.1 | 9.3 | 2.2 | 10.5 |
| Under 1 year (%) | 14.6 | 18.4 | 12.6 | 12.8 | 10.5 | 12.0 | 13.5 | 2.7 | 16.3 |
| Over 10 years (%) | 25.5 | 19.9 | 30.9 | 24.1 | 44.2 | 48.2 | 32.1 | 11.5 | 40.9 |

Notes: [a] The breakdown provided by the Czech Statistical Office differs slightly for two sub-periods, as it refers to [1] 1–3 years and [2] 3–5 years. The corresponding figures for average and standard deviation for these two categories therefore do not include Czech data. [b] Data are for 1998. For average tenure: EU, the United States and Japan; for the distribution of employment by tenure: EU and the United States.   .. = not available.

Sources: Eurostat; Czech data from the *Statistical Yearbook of the Czech Republic*, 2000.

more and perhaps better job opportunities elsewhere. This also tends to reduce average job tenure. At the same time, however, the incidence of dismissals declines, which has the contrary effect of lengthening tenure. In industrialized countries, the "shortening" effect of voluntary quits offsets the "lengthening" effect of reduced dismissals, thereby generating a countercyclical pattern of job tenure, i.e. a decline in tenure during economic upswings (see Auer and Cazes, 2000).

The opposite appears true of transition economies, where average tenure seems to decrease during downturns because the reduction in voluntary quits does not offset the increase in dismissals due to major, transition-induced structural changes. It is therefore important to consider not only the distribution and composition of these inflows into and outflows from employment and the relationship between voluntary and involuntary quits, but also whether or not the "core" group of workers changes over time, as reflected in the distribution of job tenure. Moreover, labour market institutions also need to be taken into account, notably as regards dismissals. For example, while dismissals are typically subject to an explicit or implicit rule of seniority (last in, first out), early retirement schemes may produce the opposite effect. Other influences include changes in social policy, such as the extension of parental leave in some countries or the abolition of guaranteed redeployment for workers made redundant.

The shortness of average job tenure in Estonia, for example, should be analysed in light of the very high separation rates that prevailed until 1994 and the high proportion of workers with less than one year's tenure (18.4 per cent in 1999). Slovenia's high average tenure is probably due to the low level of both separations and short-term turnover, associated with rather strict rules governing dismissals. In Poland, similarly long job tenure may be explained by the large size and stability of the agricultural sector and the existence of strong insider power in Polish firms (which, to a certain extent, is also the case in Slovenia). Cross-country differences are more pronounced when the distribution of employment across job-tenure classes is considered, especially as regards the share of workers with long tenures.[9] There are significant differences in the proportion of workers with ten or more years of tenure between, say, Slovenia and Poland (48.2 and 44.3 per cent, respectively) and Estonia and the Czech Republic (19.9 and 25.5 per cent, respectively). In the latter two countries, the share of workers with long tenure is indeed particularly low, even below the corresponding figure for the United States (25.8 per cent in 1998). These striking differences can be partly explained by the sectoral distribution of job tenure (see below).

## 4.2.2   Changes in average tenure over time

While it is interesting to ponder the differences between countries with regard to job tenure and their respective balances of employment stability and flexibility, the more relevant question for an assessment of labour market change is that of the evolution of tenure over time. The relevant data for the 1990s are available only for the Czech Republic, Poland and Slovenia; for the other three countries in tables 4.5a and 4.5b, only data for the last two to three years can be provided.

The available data show that job stability followed different patterns at country level over the past decade. In the Czech Republic, average tenure tends to be positively correlated with economic growth: after declining in the period of initial structural changes brought about by economic reforms, it increased in the more buoyant 1994–97 period and then declined again slightly during the economic recession that followed. In contrast, it has increased after an initial decline in Poland and shows a tendency to decline in Slovenia (table 4.5a).

An analysis of job-tenure data by sex indicates that women tend to be disproportionately affected by economic crisis in Estonia and in the Czech Republic.

---

[9] Standard deviation is particularly high for the two groups of workers with long tenure.

Table 4.5a  Average job tenure in selected transition countries, 1993–99 (years)

| Country | 1993 | 1994 | 1995 | 1996 | 1997 | 1998 | 1999 |
|---|---|---|---|---|---|---|---|
| Czech Republic | 8.4 | 8.1 | 8.3 | 8.4 | 8.5 | 8.2 | 8.2 |
| Estonia | .. | .. | .. | .. | 7.1 | 7.0 | 6.9 |
| Hungary | .. | .. | .. | .. | 8.3 | 8.6 | 8.8 |
| Lithuania | .. | .. | .. | .. | .. | 7.7 | 7.6 |
| Poland | .. | 11.5 | .. | 11.1 | 11.4 | 11.5 | 11.9 |
| Slovenia | 12.6 | 12.6 | 12.3 | 12.2 | 12.0 | 12.4 | 12.1 |

Table 4.5b  Average job tenure by sex in selected transition countries, 1993–99 (years)

| Country | 1993 | | 1994 | | 1995 | | 1996 | | 1997 | | 1998 | | 1999 | |
|---|---|---|---|---|---|---|---|---|---|---|---|---|---|---|
| | M | F | M | F | M | F | M | F | M | F | M | F | M | F |
| Czech Republic | 8.5 | 8.2 | 8.3 | 7.9 | 8.3 | 8.2 | 8.4 | 8.3 | 8.4 | 8.3 | 8.3 | 8.0 | 8.4 | 7.8 |
| Estonia | .. | .. | .. | .. | .. | .. | .. | .. | 6.4 | 7.9 | 6.4 | 7.7 | 6.3 | 7.6 |
| Hungary | .. | .. | .. | .. | .. | .. | .. | .. | 8.0 | 8.6 | 8.3 | 9.0 | 8.6 | 9.1 |
| Lithuania | .. | .. | .. | .. | .. | .. | .. | .. | .. | .. | 6.9 | 8.5 | 6.9 | 8.3 |
| Poland | .. | .. | 11.1 | 12.0 | .. | .. | 10.6 | 11.7 | 10.8 | 12.1 | 11.0 | 12.1 | 11.4 | 12.3 |
| Slovenia | 12.6 | 12.6 | 12.3 | 12.9 | 12.0 | 12.6 | 12.0 | 12.3 | 11.5 | 12.5 | 11.9 | 12.9 | 11.7 | 12.5 |

Note:  .. = not available.

Sources: Eurostat; for the Czech Republic and Slovenia national data; for Poland, Lehmann and Wadsworth, 2000.

In the latter country, for example, there has been a significant decline in women's average tenure since the economic recession of 1997, while average tenure for men remained stable over the entire decade (table 4.5b). A recent study of labour mobility in the Czech Republic found sex and education to be strong determinants of individual tenures. Female and less-educated workers have a higher probability of losing their jobs and are less likely to be hired if they are unemployed or out of the labour force (Sorm and Terrell, 1999). In Poland, job stability has tended to follow similar patterns for men and women, even if their respective average tenures differ. This contrasts with Slovenia, where women's average tenure remained almost constant, while men's declined by almost one year over the decade.

A remarkable feature of most of the transition countries is that the job tenure of male workers tends to be shorter than that of female workers, except in the Czech Republic (where the pattern is reversed, albeit with a small male/female differential).

This clearly reflects the lower labour turnover of women compared to men, which may be partly explained by women's stronger attachment to their jobs for fear of re-employment difficulties. Women are also less mobile because they are over-represented in the low-paid but more secure public sector, while men are generally more attracted to new job opportunities in expanding sectors that have emerged with economic reforms.

As noted earlier, the evolution of the distribution of employment by job tenure over time is very important for identifying any changes in employment stability. Though the required data are available only for the Czech Republic, Poland and Slovenia (see table 4.6), these reveal wide diversity across countries. In particular, the share of workers with short tenures in the first years of economic transition was much higher in the Czech Republic than it was in Poland or Slovenia. This goes against the widespread view that the Czech Republic's relatively low unemployment is related mainly to delayed enterprise restructuring which, in turn, encouraged labour hoarding. This is only partly true. The large portion of workers with tenures under one year shows that labour mobility and flexibility were actually high until 1994 and contributed significantly to the smooth redeployment of workers to expanding sectors offering better jobs. With economic stabilization, however, that proportion declined markedly, from about 22 per cent at the end of 1993 to 13.3 per cent at the end of 1997. In 1998, following the economic recession, the proportion of workers who changed their jobs rose rather sharply again. In Poland and particularly in Slovenia, by contrast, the proportion of short-tenured workers increased over most of the period reviewed, though it has recently declined in all three countries (most markedly in Poland, from 15.7 per cent in 1997 to 10.5 per cent in 1999).

The percentage of workers with less than one year's tenure includes not only new hires and new labour market entrants (mainly school leavers), but also workers on temporary assignments. In Slovenia, for example, the significant increase in the proportion of short-tenured workers after 1996 partly reflects a substantial increase in the use of temporary workers (as will be seen below). Indeed, the pattern observed in Slovenia suggests that this country has made considerable progress towards increasing labour market flexibility and moderating rigidities, as witnessed also by the decline in its particularly high percentage of workers with long tenure. Interestingly, the proportion of long-tenured workers declined in the Czech Republic as well while, surprisingly, it increased in Poland after 1997 despite the strong structural changes associated with the restructuring of large enterprises in the coalmining and steel industries.

These developments over time have to be analysed with care because changing patterns of job tenure may also reflect changes in the age structure of the working population and in the economic cycle. As workers change jobs more often when they are young[10] and since employers tend to fire young workers first in periods of economic slump, an economy with a relatively young working population will

---

[10] Young people seek to diversify their working experience; their career moves are also often associated with promotion, more responsibility and higher financial reward.

Table 4.6  Distribution of employment by job tenure for the Czech Republic, Poland and Slovenia, 1993–99 (percentages)

| Country | 1993 | 1994 | 1995 | 1996 | 1997 | 1998 | 1999 |
|---|---|---|---|---|---|---|---|
| **Czech Republic**[1] | | | | | | | |
| Under 6 months | 11.0 | 10.9 | 8.4 | 7.6 | 7.0 | 7.0 | 6.3 |
| 6 to 11 months | 11.2 | 8.4 | 7.7 | 7.1 | 6.3 | 9.1 | 8.3 |
| Under 1 year | 22.2 | 19.3 | 16.1 | 14.7 | 13.3 | 16.1 | 14.6 |
| 10 to 20 years | 16.0 | 14.3 | 14.1 | 14.0 | 13.8 | 12.2 | 12.3 |
| Over 20 years | 16.7 | 15.8 | 15.4 | 15.0 | 14.9 | 14.0 | 13.2 |
| Over 10 years | 32.7 | 30.1 | 29.5 | 29.0 | 28.7 | 26.2 | 25.5 |
| **Poland** | | | | | | | |
| Under 1 year | .. | 13.8 | .. | 14.3 | 15.7 | 14.6 | 10.5 |
| 10 to 20 years | .. | 22.1 | .. | 20.6 | 20.0 | 20.1 | 22.3 |
| Over 20 years | .. | 24.9 | .. | 23.8 | 21.0 | 21.4 | 22.0 |
| Over 10 years | .. | 47.0 | .. | 44.4 | 41.0 | 41.5 | 44.3 |
| **Slovenia** | | | | | | | |
| Under 1 year | 5.2 | 10.4 | 11.7 | 9.8 | 12.6 | 13.5 | 12.0 |
| 10 to 20 years | 29.2 | 28.4 | 28.0 | 26.5 | 24.3 | 23.7 | 23.6 |
| Over 20 years | 24.9 | 26.1 | 25.2 | 25.5 | 25.7 | 25.2 | 24.6 |
| Over 10 years | 54.1 | 54.5 | 53.2 | 52.0 | 50.0 | 48.9 | 48.2 |

Notes: [1] Czech data for 1993, 1994, 1995, 1996 and 1997: December to February of the following year; for 1998 and 1999: October to December. .. = not available.

Sources: Eurostat for Slovenia national data; Eurostat for Czech Republic national data; for Poland Lehmann and Wadsworth, 2000.

exhibit shorter average tenures than an economy with an ageing population. Conversely, since older workers have longer tenure on average, population ageing could mask a shift towards less secure employment.

The transition countries have indeed witnessed significant demographic changes with rather conflicting effects on their labour markets. On the one hand, all these countries are confronted with population ageing.[11] While older workers tend to have more stable employment, once they lose their job they find it difficult to be re-employed. Moreover, those at or close to retirement age have often been forced to

---

[11] The share of persons aged above 45 increased from 34.4 per cent in 1990 to 39.7 per cent in 1999 in the Czech Republic, from 29.8 per cent to 34.9 per cent in the same period in Poland, and from 36.8 per cent in 1991 to 38.2 per cent in 1999 in Slovenia.

quit their jobs – although recent pension reforms have introduced a gradual extension of retirement age and partly compensated for a decline in the participation rates of this age group. On the other hand, the transition countries have recorded a significant increase in their labour supply due to young people and women entering the labour market in large numbers in the first half of the 1990s.[12] With the exception of Poland, this phenomenon had already tailed off by 1995.[13] The point is that demographic factors may have played a part in increasing the proportion of short tenures in the three countries within the first years of economic reform and in reducing it later on. However, the sharp decline in the proportion of longer job tenures is evidence of growing employment instability for older workers. The process of population ageing will thus become an important factor in future labour supply, contributing to labour shortages and mismatches in the labour market.

The business cycle also affects average job tenure. As mentioned earlier, the transition countries, unlike the advanced industrialized countries, tend to display a pro-cyclical pattern of average job tenure. The lengthening of job tenure observed in recent years thus seems to reflect the economic stabilization and recovery that have taken place since the transition crisis. And when the Czech economy went into recession after 1997, the acceleration of structural changes had a negative impact on average job tenure; this too was in line with the pro-cyclical pattern of tenure. Since 1998, however, the relationship between average tenure and economic growth seems to have been reversed in Poland and Slovenia.

### 4.2.3   Tenure profiles of different categories of workers

Table 4.7 presents average tenure by sex, age group, sector, occupation and educational attainment. As pointed out above, the unweighted averages across countries show that women have longer tenure than men (except in the Czech Republic) and that tenure increases sharply with age. There is also little difference between countries as to the tenure of young workers: the average is about two years (slightly above the industrialized country average), although Estonia, Poland and Slovenia have a slightly lower average tenure for this age group. This probably does not reflect labour supply behaviour, as youth unemployment rates are significantly higher than the average rates in these countries.[14] These countries also tend to be characterized by higher shares of part-time and temporary youth employment.

The average tenure of workers over 45 for the six countries is below the average job tenure of the advanced industrialized countries (15 years against 18 years). Yet

---

[12] Because of lower fertility rates, fewer women are on extended childcare or parental leave beyond statutory maternity leave.

[13] The share of persons aged between 15 and 24 increased from 14.9 per cent of total population over age 15 in 1990 to 16.7 per cent in 1995, and declined afterwards to 15.5 per cent in 1999. In Slovenia the analogous figures are, respectively, 14.7, 15.8 and 14.8 per cent. Only in Poland has the proportion of this age group in the population aged over 15 constantly increased over the 1990s – from 14.1 per cent in 1990 to 16.9 per cent in 1999.

[14] The unemployment rate for young people aged 15–19 was 45.6 per cent in Poland in 1999 and 29.7 per cent for those aged 20–24 (*Statistical Yearbook of Poland*, 2000).

there is considerable variation across countries for workers aged over 45 years: in Estonia, their average tenure was about 10 years in 1999 (compared to 11 years in the United States), but it was twice as high in Poland and Slovenia. First, this heterogeneity across countries reflects the extent of the structural changes that took place, particularly during the initial phase of reform. Second, it reveals inter-country differences in employment protection for older workers – depending on trade union power, seniority rules and employers' preferences – and shows how labour market pressures have been alleviated at the expense of older workers. In all the countries reviewed, the labour force participation rates of older workers declined sharply after the introduction of early retirement schemes (except in the Baltic States), coupled with pressures on working pensioners to withdraw from the labour market and on many older workers to give up economic activity (usually through early retirement, invalidity pensions or other social welfare provisions).[15]

Job tenure also varies considerably across industries: the longest tenures are found in mining and quarrying, and electricity, gas and water supply. Workers in the education and health sectors also have longer tenures (around 11 years in 1999). The fact that the latter two sectors mainly employ women could partly explain why female tenure was longer than male tenure. The agricultural sector also tends to be characterized by long tenure. In this case, however, the data should be interpreted with caution, as they reflect great diversity across countries (24 years in Slovenia against seven years in the Baltic States, for example). In Slovenia, there was little change of ownership in agriculture, while in other countries agricultural cooperatives were dissolved or transformed into joint-stock companies, limited liability companies or cooperatives of farmers (such as former state-farm workers), leading to extensive job changes even for workers who continued to do the same work.[16]

The shortest job tenures are generally found in expanding industries such as financial intermediation, the tourism sector (with only 4.7 years on average in hotels and restaurants in 1999) and business support services. Private household workers as well as those in wholesale and retail trade (which tends to employ a large number of young people) are also characterized by short average tenures. This breakdown by sector does reveal some similarities with the patterns identified in the advanced industrialized countries (see Auer and Cazes, 2000). However, so-called small-scale privatization, together with the restitution of nationalized property and the development of small enterprises initiated by economic reforms, accelerated changes in job-tenure patterns in sectors such as community and personal services, trade, hotels and, to some extent, also in construction. Inter-country differences in length of tenure in manufacturing reflected the extent of structural changes by country connected with actual privatization (as opposed to the initially formal privatization that took place in, say, the Czech Republic) and economic cycle (except for Slovenia).

---

[15] Interestingly, the decline in the participation rates was more profound in the case of men over 45 than it was among women in the same age group, for all the transition countries analysed; the only exception is the Czech Republic.

[16] Unfortunately, these data were not available for Poland, but considering its large number of family farms, one may assume that its agriculture sector is characterized by long average tenure as well (on job tenure by occupation, see below).

Table 4.7    Average job tenure by sex, age, sector, occupation and education,
selected transition countries, 1999 (years)

| | Czech Republic[1] | Estonia | Hungary | Lithuania | Poland | Slovenia | Average | Standard deviation |
|---|---|---|---|---|---|---|---|---|
| Total | 9.0 | 6.9 | 8.8 | 7.6 | 11.9 | 12.1 | 9.4 | 2.1 |
| Men | 9.3 | 6.3 | 8.6 | 6.9 | 11.4 | 11.7 | 9.0 | 2.1 |
| Women | 8.8 | 7.6 | 9.1 | 8.3 | 12.3 | 12.5 | 9.8 | 2.3 |
| *Age group* | | | | | | | | |
| 15–24 | 2.5 | 2.1 | 2.6 | 2.3 | 2.1 | 1.9 | 2.2 | 0.3 |
| 25–44 | 7.2 | 5.5 | 7.6 | 5.8 | 8.6 | 9.3 | 7.3 | 1.5 |
| 45 + | 13.9 | 10.1 | 13.6 | 12.3 | 19.0 | 20.8 | 14.9 | 4.1 |
| *Sector* | | | | | | | | |
| Agriculture, hunting and forestry | 12.9 | 7.1 | 10.6 | 6.8 | .. | 24.6 | 12.4 | 6.5 |
| Fishing | 5.4 | 8.2 | 8.9 | 5.9 | .. | 4.3 | 6.5 | 1.7 |
| Mining and quarrying | 13.9 | 13.1 | 11.4 | 11.2 | .. | 13.1 | 12.5 | 1.1 |
| Manufacturing | 10.1 | 7.0 | 9.1 | 9.2 | .. | 11.8 | 9.4 | 1.6 |
| Electricity, gas and water supply | 11.7 | 10.8 | 12.2 | 10.8 | .. | 13.4 | 11.8 | 1.0 |
| Construction | 7.0 | 5.0 | 6.2 | 6.2 | .. | 10.1 | 6.9 | 1.7 |
| Wholesale and retail trade; repair of motor vehicles, motorcycles and personal and household goods | 5.4 | 4.2 | 6.2 | 4.0 | .. | 9.0 | 5.8 | 1.8 |
| Hotels and restaurants | 4.5 | 2.9 | 5.2 | 4.0 | .. | 6.8 | 4.7 | 1.3 |
| Transport, storage and communication | 11.6 | 7.6 | 11.1 | 7.4 | .. | 11.7 | 9.9 | 2.0 |
| Financial intermediation | 6.7 | 4.6 | 6.8 | 4.4 | .. | 9.6 | 6.4 | 1.9 |
| Real estate, renting and business activities | 6.4 | 5.4 | 6.2 | 7.0 | .. | 6.7 | 6.3 | 0.6 |
| Public administration and defence; compulsory social security | 9.4 | 5.8 | 8.9 | 6.6 | .. | 9.9 | 8.1 | 1.6 |
| Education | 12.9 | 10.4 | 11.6 | 11.3 | .. | 11.9 | 11.6 | 0.8 |

*cont.*

| | Czech Republic[1] | Estonia | Hungary | Lithuania | Poland | Slovenia | Average | Standard deviation |
|---|---|---|---|---|---|---|---|---|
| *cont.* | | | | | | | | |
| Health and social work | 10.4 | 10.1 | 11.3 | 10.3 | .. | 12.4 | 10.9 | 0.8 |
| Other community, social and personal service | 7.1 | 7.6 | 8.2 | 8.2 | .. | 10.0 | 8.2 | 1.0 |
| Private household and employed persons | 1.6 | 1.6 | 5.6 | 1.5 | .. | 5.1 | 3.1 | 1.9 |
| *Occupation* | | | | | | | | |
| Armed forces | 14.7 | 3.6 | 10.2 | 7.6 | .. | .. | 9.1 | 4.7 |
| Legislators, senior officials and managers | 8.9 | 7.4 | 10.4 | 8.5 | 10.4 | 9.5 | 9.2 | 1.2 |
| Professionals | 10.3 | 9.6 | 10.8 | 11.3 | 11.4 | 10.3 | 10.6 | 0.7 |
| Technicians and associated professionals | 10.1 | 7.8 | 10.1 | 8.6 | 11.6 | 10.9 | 9.8 | 1.4 |
| Clerks | 8.9 | 7.5 | 9.5 | 8.9 | 10.7 | 11.3 | 9.5 | 1.4 |
| Service workers, shop and market sales workers | 5.9 | 4.4 | 6.2 | 5.1 | 6.0 | 9.2 | 6.1 | 1.6 |
| Skilled agricultural and fishery workers | 10.1 | 6.4 | 8.7 | 6.0 | 21.8 | 25.2 | 13.0 | 8.3 |
| Craft and related trade workers | 9.1 | 6.4 | 8.5 | 7.1 | 9.6 | 10.3 | 8.5 | 1.5 |
| Plant and machine operators and assemblers | 10.2 | 7.5 | 9.1 | 8.4 | 10.3 | 11.9 | 9.6 | 1.5 |
| Elementary occupations | 8.0 | 5.5 | 6.6 | 5.7 | 7.7 | 10.2 | 7.3 | 1.8 |
| *Education* | | | | | | | | |
| Low | 10.0 | 6.9 | 8.8 | 7.0 | 19.7 | 18.6 | 11.8 | 5.8 |
| Medium | 8.9 | 6.4 | 8.4 | 6.4 | 10.2 | 10.5 | 8.5 | 1.8 |
| High | 9.8 | 7.9 | 10.3 | 8.8 | 10.6 | 9.6 | 9.5 | 1.0 |

Notes:[1] Data for the Czech Republic cannot be compared with the previous figures, as they only refer here to workers with permanent contracts. Data for sector and occupation use the national classification systems and are regrouped to correspond approximately to NACE (Rev.1) and ISCO-88. .. = not available.

Source: Eurostat.

The distribution of tenure by occupation is consistent with the analysis by sector. Generally speaking, skilled white-collar occupations (professionals and technicians, for example) have the longest job tenures, while semi-skilled and unskilled manual jobs and lower-skilled white-collar occupations (such as service workers, shop and market sales workers) have shorter tenures. Particularly long tenures are found among "skilled agricultural and fishery workers" in Poland (22 years) and Slovenia (25 years). This can be attributed to the fact that no significant changes in ownership in agriculture have taken place in these two countries, contrary to what happened elsewhere. It also reflects the fact that agriculture comprises a large proportion of low-skilled and stable jobs typically performed by older workers (this factor is particularly strong in Poland). Interestingly, the patterns of job tenure by industry and occupation are dependent on the nature of occupations, and thus similar across countries.[17]

Average job tenures by educational attainment, however, do not show a consistent pattern across countries. In Estonia, Hungary and Lithuania, highly educated workers have longer tenures than workers with lower education, whereas the reverse holds true of the Czech Republic, Poland and Slovenia (table 4.7). The explanation may be that while the first three countries experienced more redundancies among less-educated workers as a result of downsizing in manufacturing and agriculture, the other three countries delayed enterprise restructuring in industry. The resulting pattern of tenure may seem surprising, as less-qualified people might be expected to have less job stability. Yet empirical research based on a disaggregated analysis of the evolution of job tenure found results consistent with the previous findings for Western countries.[18]

Another interesting breakdown refers to average tenure by enterprise size, as shown in table 4.8. The distribution suggests a consistent picture across countries: job tenure clearly increases with enterprise size in almost all of the countries under review. The employees of larger establishments (enterprises with 50 or more workers) have significantly longer job tenure (11.4 years on average in 1999) than those in establishments with fewer than ten workers (7.2 years on average). The influence of enterprise size does not fit this pattern in Poland: it is 9.5 years for enterprises with fewer than ten employees, 7.2 years for enterprises with 11 to 19 employees, 9.2 years for enterprises with 20 to 49 employees, and 13 years for enterprises with 50 or more employees.[19]

Evidence from Western European countries suggests that employees stay longer in larger establishments and in production sectors (Bellman, Bender and Hornsteiner, 2000; Burgess, Pacelli and Rees, 1997). In the transition countries, the pattern may also be partly explained by the fact that enforcement of EPL is much weaker in very small firms, which thus feel less constrained in deciding to dismiss workers. Another possible factor is that many of these enterprises were established only recently. Generally, these findings are largely in line with the experience of Western European countries.

---

[17] This is consistent with earlier findings on the OECD countries (see Auer and Cazes, 2000).

[18] For example, Burgess and Rees (1998) found that post-compulsory educational qualifications in the United Kingdom are associated with shorter job tenures for both men and women.

[19] Figures for Poland should be interpreted with caution, as the distribution is likely to be biased by the agricultural sector.

Table 4.8   Average tenure by enterprise size, selected transition countries, 1999 (years)

| No. of employees | Czech Republic | Estonia | Hungary | Lithuania | Poland | Slovenia | Average | Standard deviation |
|---|---|---|---|---|---|---|---|---|
| 1 – 10 | 7.3 | 5.0 | 6.5 | 4.4 | 9.5 | 10.4 | 7.2 | 2.4 |
| 11 – 19 | 8.2 | 5.5 | 7.7 | 6.0 | 7.2 | .. | 6.9 | 1.2 |
| 20 – 49 | 9.4 | 6.9 | 8.8 | 8.2 | 9.2 | 10.6 | 8.8 | 1.2 |
| 50 + | 11.9 | 9.1 | 10.8 | 10.2 | 13.0 | 13.3 | 11.4 | 1.7 |

Note: .. = not available.

Source: Eurostat.

## 4.2.4   Labour turnover and job tenure

Section 4.1 identified a tendency towards a countercyclical pattern of labour turnover in the selected transition countries – particularly those more advanced in economic reforms – while this section has so far shown average job tenure to be pro-cyclical. These findings are compatible with the argument that an increase in labour turnover tends to shorten average tenure, while slower turnover means labour market stabilization and a lengthening of job tenure. However, this consistent picture for each of the countries studied is at odds with the findings of a cross-country comparison. From the above argument, it should indeed follow that the higher a country's labour turnover, the shorter its average job tenure. However, a comparison of tables 4.1, 4.4 and 4.5a (data for Hungary and Lithuania were unavailable for table 4.1) conflicts with this logic. The ranking of countries by rate of labour turnover in the second half of the 1990s starts with the Czech Republic (lowest), followed by Slovenia, Estonia and Poland (highest). Yet the ranking by average job tenure is Slovenia (longest), followed by Poland, the Czech Republic and Estonia.

Two factors may explain this apparent paradox. The first is that Poland and Slovenia seem to have highly segmented labour markets. On the one hand, both countries have a large proportion of workers with long tenures – almost unaffected by economic transition as far as their employment is concerned – which increases these countries' average job-tenure figures. On the other hand, a high proportion of workers in Poland and Slovenia lost their jobs, and many of these redundant workers seem to have moved into precarious employment, resulting in much higher labour turnover for this group of workers, compared to other groups. At least for Slovenia this is clearly reflected in the high share of temporary employment (see table 3.3 in Chapter 3). Many of these workers have also become unemployed or inactive in Poland, which has not been so much the case in the Czech Republic.

The second factor is a combination of methodological differences in labour statistics across transition countries[20] and of the difficulty of obtaining reliable data on atypical forms of employment. Cross-country comparisons should therefore be interpreted with caution.

## 4.3 JOB SECURITY VERSUS JOB STABILITY

In the preceding section, job tenure was used to assess job stability. However, since average tenure is determined by both voluntary and involuntary moves, it provides ambiguous information about job security per se. Moreover, while average job tenure emphasizes the trends in stable employment, short-term jobs or labour market churning are best described by separation rates.[21] Data on outflows from employment that identify or reflect the reasons for job changes – dismissals, plant closures, voluntary quits, or retirement and other "natural" separations – are necessary to make proper inferences about job security. This is important because workers leaving voluntarily are likely to improve their well-being, whereas involuntary separations are likely to make workers worse off, especially if they face difficulties in re-entering employment. In developed countries, as explained earlier, voluntary quits are more significant determinants of fluctuations in labour turnover than are dismissals: in periods of economic upswing they become more frequent, while the incidence of dismissals is rather modest, and during economic recession they decline more sharply than redundancies increase.

### 4.3.1 Outflows from employment

Two types of data on outflows from employment are available for selected transition countries: separations by reason (usually termination by employer, voluntary separation and separation for other reasons) are shown in table 4.9, and separations by destination (exit to another job, to unemployment and to inactivity) in table 4.10. The former is based on enterprise-level data and the latter on labour force surveys.

For all the countries covered, disaggregating the separation rate by reason reveals that economic reasons in general contributed much less to total separations during the transition period than is usually believed (for a detailed presentation of these data, see Cazes and Nesporova, 2001). The proportion of separations for economic reasons increased between 1991 and 1993 – that is, in the period of strong structural shifts for the CSEE countries – but remained below 40 per cent of all separations. For this group of countries there is a clear correlation between economic fluctuations and the

---

[20] The annual data on labour turnover for Poland are calculated on the basis of quarterly data, so that multiple changes of labour market status in the course of the year are counted. This increases Poland's rate of labour turnover – particularly in respect of workers in precarious employment – compared to that for Estonia and Slovenia (which is based on data collected once a year and therefore does not include multiple changes within one year). For the Czech Republic, as already mentioned, available data underestimate actual labour turnover due to incomplete inclusion of job-to-job moves.

[21] The separation rate is the ratio of the total number of workers having left or lost their job during a given period (a month, a year) to the total number of workers in employment at the beginning of the period.

Table 4.9    Separation rates by reason of separation (percentages)

| Country | 1990 | 1991 | 1992 | 1993 | 1994 | 1995 | 1996 | 1997 | 1998 | 1999 |
|---|---|---|---|---|---|---|---|---|---|---|
| **A/ Termination by employer** | | | | | | | | | | |
| Bulgaria | 3.2 | 10.9 | 11.7 | 11.7 | 7.3 | 3.7 | 4.2 | 6.0 | 5.0 | 5.7 |
| Poland | 1.5 | 6.6 | 5.9 | 6.4 | 5.4 | 4.9 | 4.1 | 3.0 | 4.3 | .. |
| Russian Fed. | .. | .. | .. | 1.5 | 2.2 | 1.6 | .. | .. | .. | .. |
| Ukraine | .. | .. | .. | .. | .. | .. | 2.2 | 2.8 | 1.9 | 1.9 |
| **B/ Voluntary quits and other reasons for separation** | | | | | | | | | | |
| Bulgaria | 25.7 | 25.3 | 19.4 | 17.9 | 18.5 | 18.8 | 20.6 | 25.9 | 24.8 | 34.2 |
| Poland | .. | .. | 6.0 | 3.8 | 4.2 | 4.5 | 3.7 | 2.9 | 3.5 | .. |
| Russian Fed. | .. | .. | .. | 23.6 | 25.2 | 24.1 | .. | .. | .. | .. |
| Ukraine | .. | .. | .. | .. | .. | .. | 15.5 | 14.0 | 15.8 | 16.8 |
| **C/ of B/ only voluntary quits** | | | | | | | | | | |
| Poland | .. | .. | 6.0 | 3.8 | 4.2 | 4.5 | 3.7 | 2.9 | 3.5 | .. |
| Russian Fed. | .. | .. | .. | 16.3 | 17.6 | 17.6 | .. | .. | .. | .. |

Note:  .. = not available.

Source: National statistics based on establishment surveys.

proportion of redundancies, with the latter increasing in periods of economic recession (or significant economic slowdown) and declining with economic recovery. In the CIS countries, by contrast, redundancies have never accounted for more than a small fraction of total separations.

The difference between the two subregions is even more striking for voluntary quits. Although these data are available only for Poland and the Russian Federation, they show that the number of voluntary quits has always been below that of redundancies in Poland, while being the most frequent form of separations in the Russian Federation.

This difference seems to indicate that the Polish labour market is much tighter than that of the Russian Federation. Polish workers are apparently reluctant to change their job unless they already have a new one. Structural changes have increasingly been solved by measures other than redundancies (such as retirement, out-of-job training, maternity leave). In contrast, the Russian labour market would seem to offer many opportunities. However, research provides another explanation. Facing economic problems, Russian employers prefer methods other than redundancy to cut labour costs, such as administrative leave, extended maternity leave, short-time work, real wage cuts or non-payment of wages. As a rule, older workers or women with small children, especially in regions with few good job opportunities in the market, accept such solutions while relying on other sources of income. Younger workers solve the situation by quitting in the hope of finding something better. The research revealed that the actual reason for departure was economic in 83 per cent of cases (including both redundancies and quasi-voluntary quits).[22]

A steeply increasing proportion of separations other than redundancies in Bulgaria since 1997 (terminations by employers went up only slightly) could indicate that employers sought agreement with redundant workers with the aim of avoiding long notice periods or severance pay and they more often switched to temporary contracts. It is true of all the transition countries that employers prefer to agree with the redundant workers on retirement, early retirement or another form of "voluntary" departure rather than on dismissal. This solution is less costly for employers and prevents social tensions, while the workers get some income from public social funds (see also below) or at least do not have the stigma of appearing to be less productive, thereby improving their re-employment chances.

According to table 4.10, which shows separations by destination for the Czech Republic, Estonia, Hungary, Poland and Slovenia, outflows from employment to inactivity significantly exceeded outflows to unemployment. This indicates that labour market pressures were dealt with primarily at the expense of older workers, by pushing them to accept regular or early retirement (reaching retirement age does not automatically mean the termination of the contract), and of some other vulnerable groups. Also, resignations were more frequent in the initial difficult period of economic transition, while their incidence declined later. In Estonia and Slovenia the shares of withdrawals from employment to inactivity were several times higher than outflows to unemployment in the initial stage of economic reforms. For the Czech Republic, Hungary and Poland, the data before 1993 are not available but rapidly declining participation rates in this period would indicate the same tendency as in Estonia and Slovenia. While Estonia rapidly closed the gap and even reversed this relation after 1997, in the other countries under review the outflow to unemployment remained lower than to inactivity.

There are remarkable differences between the Czech Republic, Estonia, Poland and Slovenia in job-to-job moves, with rates particularly high in Estonia and above average in the Czech Republic also. In Estonia, job-to-job flows exceeded by far the other two destinations of separated workers for the whole transition period. This confirms the country's exceptionally high labour mobility supported, as mentioned earlier, by massive structural changes. The data available for the Czech Republic give similar evidence of workers' high mobility, particularly up to 1995, over the period when labour reallocation needs could be met relatively easily without long spells of unemployment. This contrasts with the situation in Poland where the incidence of direct job-to-job moves was the same as that of redundancies (and probably even lower before 1995), while that of withdrawals from employment to inactivity was

Table 4.10 Separation rates by destination of outflows from employment, selected transition countries, 1990–2000 (percentages)

| Country | 1990 | 1991 | 1992 | 1993 | 1994 | 1995 | 1996 | 1997 | 1998 | 1999 | 2000 |
|---|---|---|---|---|---|---|---|---|---|---|---|
| **Employment to unemployment (EU)** | | | | | | | | | | | |
| Czech Rep. | .. | .. | .. | 1.7 | 1.4 | 1.2 | 1.5 | 1.8 | 3.0 | .. | .. |
| Estonia | 0.7 | 1.7 | 4.9 | 5.4 | 5.1 | 4.2 | 4.8 | 4.6 | 6.0 | .. | .. |
| Hungary | .. | .. | .. | 4.7 | 2.8 | 2.8 | 2.2 | 2.2 | 1.7 | 1.4 | 1.2 |
| Poland | .. | .. | 7.9 | 8.4 | 8.1 | 6.8 | 6.2 | 5.0 | 5.0 | .. | .. |
| Slovenia | 2.3 | 4.1 | .. | 3.3 | 2.3 | 2.2 | 2.7 | 2.4 | 2.5 | 2.8 | 1.8 |
| **Employment to inactivity (EI)** | | | | | | | | | | | |
| Czech Rep. | .. | .. | .. | 5.3 | 4.3 | 5.6 | 4.0 | 3.8 | 3.7 | .. | .. |
| Estonia | 5.6 | 6.4 | 10.0 | 7.5 | 6.5 | 3.0 | 5.0 | 4.0 | 4.6 | .. | .. |
| Hungary | .. | .. | .. | 8.0 | 5.7 | 6.3 | 5.1 | 5.4 | 4.1 | 3.2 | 3.1 |
| Poland | .. | .. | 11.4 | 12.8 | 11.1 | 8.4 | 8.3 | 7.7 | 6.8 | .. | .. |
| Slovenia | 8.7 | 8.0 | .. | 6.5 | 6.2 | 5.1 | 6.9 | 7.1 | 5.9 | 7.1 | 6.3 |
| **Employment to employment (EE)** | | | | | | | | | | | |
| Czech Rep. | .. | .. | .. | 14.9 | 11.8 | 9.0 | 7.1 | 6.5 | 5.0 | .. | .. |
| Estonia | 9.7 | 12.2 | 16.5 | 17.0 | 16.1 | 9.0 | 12.2 | 9.8 | 8.4 | .. | .. |
| Poland | .. | .. | .. | .. | 6.5 | 6.4 | 10.4 | 6.0 | 5.2 | .. | .. |
| Slovenia | 5.0 | 4.9 | .. | 5.3 | 5.7 | 5.4 | .. | .. | .. | .. | .. |

Note: .. = not available.

Source: Labour force surveys.

consistently higher, particularly prior to 1996 (1996 being the only exception). Until 1995, the situation in Slovenia resembled that of Poland, with outflows from employment to inactivity exceeding job-to-job moves. After 1995, however, stricter conditions for early retirement contributed to a sharp decline in moves to inactivity.

## 4.3.2 Correlation of employment outflows with the business cycle

As explained above, demand for labour in the industrialized countries increases in periods of economic upswing. At such times, employers also tend to offer higher wages in order to attract new and more qualified workers. The latter, in turn, are more inclined to avail themselves of better job opportunities so that, besides new labour market entries and re-employment of previously unemployed persons, job-to-job moves also accelerate. In contrast, in periods of economic decline workers become more hesitant to change their jobs voluntarily for fear of eventually remaining jobless. Enterprises endeavour to cut production costs in order to maintain or restore their competitiveness, including, if necessary, by means of redundancies, early retirement schemes and other such measures to cut their workforce.

The evolution of GDP and employment outflows, including job-to-job moves, for four transition countries is shown in figure 4.2. In order to bring out the strength of the correlation between GDP growth rates and flows from employment to each destination, the corresponding correlation coefficients have been calculated as well (see table 4.10). The underlying assumption is that job-to-job moves are usually voluntary (unlike in the CIS countries, as mentioned above), while outflows from employment to unemployment are usually involuntary, which also largely applies to flows from employment to inactivity (forced withdrawals from employment, de-registration from unemployment, early retirement, etc.). One might therefore expect the incidence of job-to-job moves to be positively correlated to GDP growth and that of moves to unemployment and inactivity to be negatively correlated to it. Moreover, while job-to-job moves typically take place without much delay, employment protection rules delay involuntary moves from employment to unemployment and to inactivity. The latter flows are therefore also correlated to the GDP growth rates that preceded the employment outflow data by one year. Again, the results should be taken with caution, because the data series are rather short and incomplete, with differences between countries as far as coverage of the transition period is concerned.

Tables 4.11a and 4.11b show strong negative correlations between GDP growth and exits to inactivity for Estonia, Poland and Slovenia, even when exits to inactivity are time-lagged. In the Czech Republic, by contrast, moves from employment to inactivity seem to be pro-cyclical, though the time-lagged correlation tends to show a countercyclical pattern (similar to that observed in the other countries selected).

Also in line with expectations, outflows from employment to unemployment have a strong negative correlation with the economic cycle in the Czech Republic, Poland and Slovenia, regardless of whether the time lag is considered or not. For Estonia, however, the relationship seems to be rather weak, possibly because the results are to some extent affected by the first three or four years of the decade, when the behaviour of enterprises and workers was still strongly influenced by past practices. Indeed, administrative leave, short-time work and delays in wage payments were rather frequent at that time, while dismissals were still quite rare and open unemployment very limited. This also explains the negative correlation between GDP and job-to-job moves, as labour churning was typical of the CIS countries in that period. Labour churning in the first years of the economic transition contrasts sharply with the lower incidence of voluntary job changes in the period of economic upswing, when workers seem to have been more cautious about quitting their job.

These results are in conformity with the countercyclical pattern of labour market flows identified above, namely, higher outflows from employment in periods of depressed demand for labour and lower outflows in times of employment growth. When demand for labour increases, fewer people are made redundant or resign

Figure 4.2   GDP growth and separation rates by destination, 1990–99 (percentages)

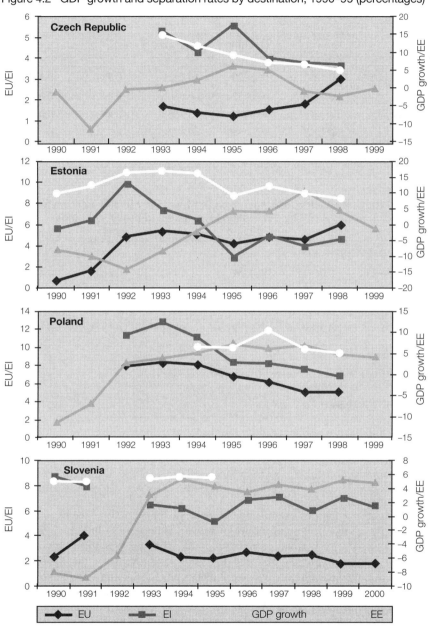

Note: EU = employment to unemployment; EI = employment to inactivity; EE = job-to-job moves.

Sources: GDP figures from UNECE, 2000, and separation rates from table 4.10.

Table 4.11a  Correlation coefficients of GDP and outflows from employment by
destination for selected transition countries

| Country | EE vs GDP | EI vs GDP | EI vs GDP (–1) | EU vs GDP | EU vs GDP (–1) |
|---|---|---|---|---|---|
| Czech Republic | 0.1291 | 0.5020 | –0.2511 | –0.7847 | –0.4126 |
| Estonia | –0.6176 | –0.8452 | –0.6607 | 0.3771 | –0.0989 |
| Hungary | .. | –0.8409 | –0.8557 | –0.8532 | –0.9032 |
| Poland | 0.1245 | –0.6721 | –0.6338 | –0.5748 | –0.5987 |
| Slovenia | 0.9318 | –0.7734 | –0.5146 | –0.5637 | –0.8728 |

Table 4.11b  Correlation coefficients of employment growth and outflows from
employment by destination for selected transition countries

| Country | EE vs GDP | EI vs GDP | EI vs GDP (–1) | EU vs GDP | EU vs GDP (–1) |
|---|---|---|---|---|---|
| Czech Republic | 0.0662 | –0.4952 | –0.1480 | –0.6502 | –0.4224 |
| Estonia | –0.5675 | 0.4528 | –0.2182 | –0.2338 | –0.5400 |
| Hungary | .. | –0.9809 | –0.9022 | –0.9803 | –0.9504 |
| Poland | –0.2389 | –0.8272 | –0.9331 | –0.7577 | –0.8806 |
| Slovenia | 0.7288 | –0.5231 | –0.0373 | –0.8173 | –0.7138 |

Note: EE is a flow from one job to another, EI a flow from employment to inactivity and EU from employment to unemployment. .. = not available.

Source: Authors' calculations based on table 4.10.

(or made to "resign voluntarily"). Conversely, when demand declines, pressures for separations either to unemployment or to inactivity increase. By and large, the signs and magnitudes of correlation between employment growth and all outflows from unemployment are very similar to those observed between GDP and outflows from employment.

Of the other countries examined here, only Slovenia confirms the hypothesis of a strong pro-cyclical pattern of job-to-job moves, although absolute changes in job-to-job flows are very small (see figure 4.2). The analysis thus suggests that separations from employment in the transition countries have mainly been the outcome of forced resignations and involuntary quits for economic reasons related to the transition crisis, structural changes and enterprises' need to reduce labour hoarding and cut labour costs. Again, this contrasts with the situation in advanced industrialized countries, where the dominant influences on overall flows seem to be voluntary quits for better jobs in periods of economic upswing and the reduction of such quits in periods of recession.

## 4.4   CONCLUSIONS

The introduction of economic and social reforms initiated long-delayed structural adjustment of the former centrally planned economies to world markets. This was facilitated by significant changes in labour legislation and labour market institutions as well. The weaknesses of newly established or refurbished institutions further enhanced adjustment flexibility for firms, which used not only direct staff cuts and real wage reductions but also shortening of working time, delayed wage payment or informal work. The latter four practices allowed enterprises merely to cut labour costs, while often contributing towards delays in the necessary restructuring of poorly performing enterprises. As a result of these reforms and the underdeveloped enforcement mechanisms, insecurity of employment and income has sharply increased in transition economies compared with the past, and ought to be compensated by institutional assistance, labour market policy and social protection.

While legislative and institutional reforms in most transition countries were influenced by the Western European approach, the outcomes of the process have been more diverse, depending on economic performance, trade union power and the importance of social dialogue as well as national culture. Hence, the Central European countries, including the Baltic States, have moved towards flexibility/protection patterns applied by EU countries, further supported by the EU accession process. In the Balkan States, adversely affected by military conflicts and economic losses due to inconsistent reforms, certain rigidities have persisted, along with weak employment and income security for workers. In the CIS countries, the adaptability of firms tends more to be constrained internally than blocked by external regulations. For historical reasons, employment protection (combined now with meagre protection of earnings) is still tied to companies, while broader labour market protection and income protection are exceedingly weak.

In the initial period of economic transformation, economic reforms stimulated restructuring connected with massive job destruction and reallocation of labour. Economic stabilization and recovery might have been expected to bring fluctuations of labour market flows roughly into line with those prevalent in industrialized countries, i.e. increasing job-to-job moves by workers seeking better jobs with higher earnings, more hires of unemployed workers or previously inactive people, and fewer redundancies and resignations. However, workers in transition countries behave differently and, even in an improved economic situation, many seem hesitant to quit their jobs voluntarily and move on to other jobs. The main reason is the heightened perception of job insecurity. Reluctance to quit voluntarily is justified by the fact that demand for labour is generally weak; many large and medium-sized companies are still or again cutting staff; small firms are often fragile. Given the rather low average wage levels of the transition countries, few workers can afford the decline in income that would come with unemployment which, for the majority, would mean falling into poverty. This is confirmed by our findings of a tendency towards a countercyclical pattern of labour turnover coupled with a pro-cyclical pattern of job tenure, which is the opposite of what happens in industrialized countries. Since 1998, however, a countercyclical pattern of job tenure seems to be emerging in Poland and Slovenia, though its sustainability has yet to be tested. In Slovenia, labour turnover too seems to have shifted towards a pro-cyclical pattern since 1997.

The analysis of the tenure profiles of different groups of workers also produced some interesting findings. First, the distribution of job tenure by industry in transition countries is very similar to that of industrialized countries. The sectoral structure of a national economy and any changes therein have a significant effect on average job tenure. A higher share of personal, production and distribution services thus tends to increase instability of employment, while a large proportion of agricultural employment or of employment in the civil and social services is conducive to longer average job tenures. Second, job tenure increases sharply with age in all the countries reviewed. In other words, the age structure of the working population also partly explains differences in job stability by country. In the 1990s, the fact that a lot of young people entered the labour market, coupled with a sharp increase in resignations and the early retirement of older workers, contributed to a general decline in job stability. Third, women tend to have slightly longer job tenures than men in the transition countries, with the exception of the Czech Republic. This confirms that sex has come to play a more decisive part in the availability and quality of employment during economic transition.

# THE IMPACT OF EPL ON LABOUR MARKET OUTCOMES: EVIDENCE FROM TRANSITION AND WESTERN INDUSTRIALIZED COUNTRIES

**5**

## 5.1    INTRODUCTION

This chapter explores the impact of EPL on aggregate labour market outcomes. EPL is understood here to refer to regulatory provisions that relate to "hiring and firing", particularly those governing unfair dismissals, termination of employment for economic reasons, severance payments, minimum notice periods, administrative authorization for dismissals, and prior consultations with trade union and/or labour administration representatives. In this chapter we do not take into consideration other types of labour market intervention or workers' protection that may affect labour market performance of the countries analysed, as this will be the subject of Chapter 6.

The purpose of this chapter is to highlight the need for analytical and statistical tools for understanding and measuring labour market flexibility and labour market performance in transition countries. It opens with a short survey of the potential benefits and costs of strict EPL in terms of its impact on aggregate employment and unemployment, as well as on their structure (i.e. certain groups of workers), and summarizes empirical evidence for 19 Western industrialized countries (hereafter "OECD-19").[1] The same analysis is then conducted in more detail for selected transition countries in the 1990s. Looking from an economic point of view rather than from a strictly legal position, the changes in employment protection and their labour market consequences are assessed in five countries – Bulgaria, the Czech Republic, Estonia, Poland and the Russian Federation. Based on this information, EPL indicators are constructed for these countries using OECD methodology (see OECD, 1994a and 1999). Finally, we provide some preliminary evidence on the link between EPL and labour market performance in these countries based on bivariate associations.

---

[1] We refer here to a group of 19 countries – Australia, Austria, Belgium, Canada, Denmark, Finland, France, Germany, Ireland, Italy, Japan, the Netherlands, New Zealand, Norway, Portugal, Spain, Sweden, the United Kingdom and the United States – for which comparative data are available. The OECD now has more members, including some from the transition countries, namely the Czech Republic, Hungary, Poland and Slovakia.

## 5.2    EXISTING WORK

### 5.2.1    Some principles governing the impact of hiring and firing rules

The strictness of the legislation protecting employment may affect both employers' and employees' decisions. The theoretical arguments for and against EPL are developed below.

The primary task of EPL is to give more employment and income security to workers, both in their current jobs and in the case of redundancy. Advance notice informs workers of redundancy plans and gives them time to search for new jobs. EPL in some countries obliges employers to offer internal redeployment if possible, and to cooperate with the trade unions and public labour market institutions in the re-employment of redundant workers, while providing financial compensation. The aim of these provisions is to strengthen workers' longer-term attachment to their jobs and employers through internal redeployment or, where this is not possible, to facilitate relatively smooth external re-employment and to moderate income loss. Stable employment prospects are there to encourage workers to undergo retraining and skills upgrading and to encourage enterprises to invest in training, thus improving productivity, the internal flexibility of the workforce and the speed of market adjustment (see Piore, 1986). Job security should also mean that workers are less resistant to the introduction of new technologies and working practices.

But stricter EPL makes redundancies in general more lengthy and costly for employers. Enterprise management should thus be forced to look for alternative solutions to dismissals, such as the enhancement of functional flexibility of the personnel through better human resource development policy and stronger motivation of workers in the framework of enterprise restructuring, technological upgrading, improved marketing strategy, and so on. Firms are thus stimulated to look for internal reserves, to invest in human resources and to constantly improve technologically and organizationally. In return, they get a loyal workforce, willing and able to constantly adapt to new technological and market challenges (see Akerlof, 1984).

Stricter EPL is also expected to provide better employment protection to certain vulnerable groups that, faced with dismissal, would have difficulty finding a new job and source of income. These groups include older workers protected by seniority rules, female employees during pregnancy and maternity leave, single parents taking care of small children, disabled workers and other groups. Employment protection thus helps mitigate discrimination against vulnerable workers, promotes their employment and helps save social welfare funds otherwise necessary for the income support of these disadvantaged groups.

In this way, stricter EPL ensuring higher job stability should enhance aggregate productivity through better enterprise adaptation, technological progress and continuous training of workers, while simultaneously ensuring better income equality and fighting against discrimination. The overall effect is expected to be improved economic performance and raised living standards (see Ichniowski, Shaw and Prennushi, 1997, and Nickell and Layard, 1999).

Potential costs of stricter EPL include first of all the widening distance between insiders, i.e. workers in regular jobs enjoying high employment security through EPL, and outsiders, i.e. those in irregular jobs (fixed-term, seasonal or any type of informal employment), as well as unemployed jobseekers, not covered by EPL. In general, for the first group of workers job tenure increases with age, while the risk of losing their job declines. In contrast, the second group faces a problem of access to regular jobs, which worsens in periods of economic volatility. In this way stricter EPL may stimulate an increase in irregular forms of employment and reduce new hiring, particularly for regular jobs. This would result in higher unemployment, and especially long-term unemployment. However, even for the first group of workers stricter EPL may bring certain disadvantages. While they are indeed better protected against job loss in general, they may be forced to accept internal redeployment to worse positions in terms of skill requirements, responsibility, status or remuneration.

Firms bear higher labour costs when stricter EPL applies, as lay-offs are combined with severance pay and other obligations in favour of redundant workers, such as assistance in re-employment and funding of labour market training. Moreover, because of more lengthy administrative procedures (advance notice, negotiations with workers' representative bodies and/or labour market institutions) the firm has to keep redundant workers on the payroll for a certain period, which again implies significant additional costs. Therefore the stricter the EPL, the more cautious firms may be in recruiting workers for regular jobs.

For society, the costs of stricter EPL may be twofold. First, the labour market duality between insiders and outsiders contributes to increasing labour market rigidity, inequality and social exclusion, requiring additional costs for their mitigation. Second, well-protected workers' fears of losing their privileges and becoming exposed to the uncertainties of the labour market prevent them from moving to more productive jobs elsewhere. But, as mentioned above, stricter EPL may also contribute towards smoother labour market adjustment, more social stability, sharing of adjustment costs between the society and the enterprise sector, and faster absorption of new technologies, with positive effects on productivity. For firms it is not always possible to make appropriate internal workforce adjustments because of a lack of investment funds, the unfavourable composition of their personnel or a difficult market situation in general, which would further diminish their market competitiveness and longer-term growth prospects. In such a situation the firm is forced to lay off workers anyway, despite the higher costs induced by EPL, and to limit new recruitments, thus increasing the level of unemployment. Moreover, the duration of unemployment rises. An increase in the number of non-competitive firms is detrimental for national economic development and prosperity in general, as it reduces resources for economic and social policy while increasing demand for funds for appropriate intervention.

This overview of the theoretical arguments indicates that EPL generates a number of effects on labour costs, employment and productivity, some favourable and some unfavourable. The net impact of these effects seems likely to vary by size of firm and type of activity and according to the economic conditions. But the theoretical models also clearly suggest that employment should be more stable and individual employment relationships more durable when EPL is stricter (i.e. in a dynamic perspective). In other words, stringent EPL reduces hiring and firing.

## 5.2.2 Evidence for Western industrialized countries

Empirical work has explored these theoretical implications using various EPL indicators and a variety of cross-sectional indicators of labour market performance. Although the literature does not provide clear-cut results, the implied behaviour of macro-indicators of labour market performance is given some support: aggregate employment and unemployment levels are not strongly affected by cross-sectional indicators of EPL stringency but are more stable. In formal empirical regressions, EPL indicators are statistically significant but their coefficient is small (see Scarpetta, 1996). Empirical studies have also looked at the effects of EPL on the stability of employment relationships from a disaggregated perspective, collecting various measures of such stability from both employees' and employers' points of view. Measures of labour turnover tend to be negatively related to EPL indicators: in Canada and the United States, for example, the intensity of labour turnover is around double that in most European countries.[2]

Some empirical work has also related labour market performance to EPL indicators and their changes over time. The results of such exercises are mixed. The OECD (1999) has made a recent overview of the impact of EPL on labour market performance, using updated indicators,[3] and in general the cross-country comparisons of EPL reveal large differences in national EPL among industrialized countries, which mostly persisted over the 1990s despite some reforms. The main findings can be summarized as follows: the OECD found a clear negative correlation between EPL strictness and the participation rate and level of employment across countries, but a positive effect on the employment rate for prime-age men (OECD, 1994b and 1999);[4] however, other studies find other explanations for this phenomenon connected more with economic and cultural differences rather than with strictness of EPL (Nickell, 1997; Bertola, Boeri and Cazes, 1999). The results of the empirical research are reviewed in box 5.1.

To summarize, empirical work provides mixed results as to the evaluation of the influence of labour market regulation on labour market performance in Western industrialized countries. It suggests that the link between theoretical and empirical

---

[2] See Bertola, Boeri and Cazes (1999). The annual rates of labour turnover (sum of separations and new hires during the sample period as a percentage of average employment levels) were 92.6 for Canada and 126.4 for the United States, against 58 for France, 62 for Germany and 68.1 for Italy in the late 1980s, while EPL was significantly stricter in these three European countries than in Canada and the United States (see table 5.1 in this chapter).

[3] The OECD (1999) has also updated and revised its EPL indicators to include regulations of collective redundancies.

[4] Possibly to the detriment of youths, women and less skilled workers.

**Box 5.1   A summary of empirical evidence on the labour market effects of stricter EPL**

According to the OECD's overview of the empirical evidence, EPL has generally been found to have little or no effect on overall unemployment, although it may affect its duration – as the length of unemployment increases with stricter EPL – and its demographic composition. Labour turnover tends to decline with stricter EPL and vice versa, but stricter EPL increases the share of direct quits from one job to another among all separations. Stricter EPL tends to increase the proportion of long-tenure jobs. Most studies confirm that stricter EPL stimulates an increase in the share of self-employment in total employment, while the effect on temporary employment and part-time employment is ambiguous. Indeed, the analysis has found no significant effect of overall EPL strictness on the share of temporary employment. Even when the overall EPL indicator is broken down into two sub-indices – one regulating regular employment and one regulating temporary employment – there is no significant effect on the incidence of temporary employment. The OECD study also shows a positive effect of liberalization of EPL on the level of temporary employment among young workers, in turn facilitating their transition from education to work, but little evidence has been found in favour of a link between strict EPL and temporary employment for other groups of workers.

The various analyses have proved a shift in the mode of labour adjustment in those countries with stricter EPL: demand fluctuations are met by adjustments of working hours rather than of employment. Strong employment protection also favours higher employment of male, prime-age, skilled workers, while encouraging lower employment levels among young people, women and less skilled workers. Other factors affecting labour market performance also need to be taken into consideration, such as collective bargaining or labour market policies, both passive and active. The results of a multivariate analysis in general confirmed some but not all of the above-mentioned findings.

First of all, no significant link between EPL strictness and overall unemployment has been found. Second, collective bargaining at the central level seems to mitigate any negative effect of stricter EPL on the level of unemployment. Third, no important effect of the replacement rate of unemployment benefits or the length of their payment on total unemployment has been revealed. In contrast, the level of spending on active labour market policies has been found to have a positive effect on the decline in unemployment; nevertheless this relationship is statistically insignificant. Fourth, while stricter EPL indeed has a positive impact on the unemployment of prime-age men, no significant correlation has been revealed between EPL strictness and higher unemployment of young people and prime-age women.

As far as employment effects are concerned, the multivariate analysis also confirmed a positive effect of stricter EPL on the employment rate of prime-age men and a negative effect on general employment as well as employment of women. However, none of these correlation coefficients was statistically significant, suggesting that EPL may have little impact on the level of employment when other factors are controlled for.

In contrast, EPL is significantly correlated with certain labour market flows across countries, such as labour turnover, inflow into unemployment, duration of unemployment and the share of long-term unemployed. The stricter the EPL, the lower the labour turnover, the higher the inflow into unemployment, the longer the duration of unemployment and the higher the proportion of long-term unemployment in total joblessness. The OECD report has also found that it is EPL concerning regular employment which is more important for these latter relationships, while legislation on temporary employment is important in the case of inflows into unemployment and duration of unemployment (but only jointly with EPL on regular employment). A multivariate analysis showed a stronger negative correlation between EPL strictness (concerning both regular and temporary employment) and the inflow rate into unemployment, and a positive correlation between EPL strictness and the duration of unemployment. Thus, the impact of EPL seems to be much greater on the dynamics and composition of unemployment than on its level.

Source: OECD, 1999, Ch. 2.

results is tenuous and ambiguous, though this may partly be explained by the elusive and complex nature of available measures of EPL, and of the EPL concept itself. However, despite their imperfections, EPL indicators are necessary for conducting empirical research. It is therefore important to develop similar analytical and statistical tools for the transition countries, bearing these caveats in mind. This is the purpose of the next sections.

## 5.3 DEVELOPMENT OF EPL OVER THE1990S: A CROSS-COUNTRY COMPARISON IN CEE COUNTRIES

Under the centrally planned economic system, workers enjoyed a fairly high degree of employment protection in their jobs. In general, the Labour Code did not allow enterprises to lay off workers for economic reasons. In (rather rare) cases of enterprise restructuring or relocation connected with the abolition of certain jobs, the enterprise was obliged to offer another job internally (combined with internal retraining if necessary) to the workers concerned. This was usually to be agreed with the worker and the trade union organization, and supplemented by compensation for hardship caused by the job transfer. Where internal redeployment was not possible, labour departments of local authorities had to find for these workers other jobs of similar quality, skill requirements and level of remuneration, as under the policy of full employment it was the State's responsibility to provide employment to all able-bodied persons of working age.

Employment protection in concrete jobs was so strong that, for example, women returning after extended maternity leave (up to three years in a number of transition countries) had not only guaranteed employment with the same employer but also guaranteed return to their previous job. Unless the reason for employment termination was a criminal offence or a serious breach of labour rules, the latter termination requiring approval by the trade union, the enterprise could not end the employment contract other than by agreement with the worker. Conversely, if the worker wished to leave the enterprise, unless the reason was among those listed in the Labour Code as legal reasons for regular employment termination (such as change of residence or under-utilization of education) the worker had to reach an agreement with the enterprise or be penalized by an extended notice period. The negative effect of the workforce stabilization policy, combined with the low level and limited differentiation of wages, was extreme labour rigidity, inefficient labour allocation and a low level of labour productivity.

The need for rapid structural adjustment of the transition economies after the introduction of economic and social reforms was reflected in profound amendments to national EPL immediately thereafter. The objective was to facilitate workforce adjustment for firms in order to make enterprises more flexible and economically competitive, while guaranteeing solid employment protection comparable with that prevailing in developed market economies. In reality, it meant substantial moderation of workers' protection in general, made possible through the weakening of trade union power. Over the 1990s, EPL was amended several times after heated discussions with the social partners, resulting in the re-tightening of employment protection in some countries and its further moderation in others. Nevertheless, the differences among the transition countries persist. This chapter presents a cross-country comparison of national EPL in five transition countries, Bulgaria, the Czech Republic, Estonia, Poland and the Russian Federation, based on the expertise of national lawyers (see Beleva and Tzanov, 2001; Arro et al., 2001; Kwiatkowski, Socha and Sztanderska, 2001; Tchetvernina et al., 2001; and Večerník, 2001).

## 5.3.1 Permanent employment

All five selected transition countries have incorporated into their national EPL the possibility of redundancy for economic reasons, including financial problems, bankruptcy, and complete or partial liquidation of the enterprise, and as a result of changes in production, production technology and structure of the enterprise. In these cases the redundant workers enjoy protection in the form of a notice period combined with severance pay. Other reasons for employment termination with notice include long-term sick leave, unsatisfactory work performance due to health problems or because of inadequate qualifications, and refusal to relocate with the enterprise or of one of its parts. In some countries, such as Bulgaria and Estonia, age and eligibility for retirement are also valid reasons for an employer to terminate with notice, while in other countries this is unlawful.

The countries, however, differ in the length of notice given (which may or may not depend on seniority and on the reason for employment termination), the level of severance pay, the existence of protection for certain vulnerable social groups, and other obligations of employers to redundant workers. The countries also vary in terms of the third-party involvement, which may extend the effective notice period. In addition, some countries have special rules for collective dismissals while others do not.

In Bulgaria, for example, the minimum notice period for individual terminations is uniformly set at 30 days, which may be extended upon agreement up to three months. There is no obligation for employers to inform a third party – be it a trade union or labour market institution – about redundancy. The only exception is the termination of trade union officials, for whom the consent of the trade union organization is requested. Dismissals of workers during their annual or sick leave, redundancies for economic reasons or for inadequate qualifications (including due to changes in job description), and dismissals of pregnant women, women with children below the age of three, wives of conscripts and disabled persons can take place only with the consent of the labour inspector responsible. Severance pay is set at two average monthly wages for workers with job tenure below ten years; however, those with job tenure of more than ten years with the same employer receive six months' wages. This significant difference in favour of long-serving employees may work against them, as employers may opt for terminating or changing their contracts before the ten years of service are complete in order to avoid this additional cost. In the case of unfair dismissal, the worker is reinstated in his or her job and gets compensation of up to six months' wages. The notion of collective redundancy is not precisely specified in Bulgarian labour legislation; the procedures are very similar to those for individual redundancy. However, the employer must inform the local authority, the local body for tripartite cooperation and the local labour office, of an intended mass lay-off 60 days in advance. If the total number of redundancies exceeds 150, the information has to be delivered to the central office of the PES. Redundant workers can also opt for a lump sum of BGL1,000 instead of monthly unemployment benefits and they can collect another BGL1,000 if they decide to start their own business or accept a new job.

Poland also differentiates workers by their seniority in redundancies. Workers with less than six months' service get a two-week notice period, those with service between six months and three years receive one month's notice, and those employed for more than three years receive three months' notice. Lay-offs justified by enterprise liquidation, bankruptcy and staff reduction allow employers the option to agree with the employee to shorten the worked notice period to one month and pay off whatever part of the notice remains. The employer is obliged to inform the trade union about the intended redundancy (except for redundancy due to liquidation or bankruptcy of the enterprise). If the union does not give its agreement, the matter is submitted to a higher-level trade union body. This requirement may protract employment termination and make it more costly for the employer. Employment cannot be terminated for pregnant women and women on maternity leave, persons on sick leave up to three months (for those with service of less than six months) or up to six months (for workers employed for more than six months) and persons retiring in less than two years. This restriction is not valid, however, when the enterprise is in the process of bankruptcy or liquidation. Apart from payment in lieu of notice as described above, no severance pay is given to redundant workers. Poland has no special arrangement for collective redundancy.

The Czech Republic, by contrast, does not have any seniority concessions. The notice period is two months for all workers regardless of their age and length of employment with the same employer, and only when the staff cuts are the result of economic or organizational changes is the period three months. The employer is obliged to discuss any intended redundancy with the trade union; however, the consent of trade unions is necessary only for their own officials. In addition, if redundancy is due to the enterprise closure, economic difficulties or organizational changes or dismissal is a result of a worker's long-term inability to comply with his/her work tasks, the employer is required to inform the local PES and cooperate in the redeployment. If the worker does not meet job performance requirements, he or she can be dismissed only after having received a warning in the previous 12 months. Single parents with children below the age of 15, disabled workers and those with occupational diseases cannot have their contract terminated unless the employer ensures their new employment. Severance pay is also uniform for all workers – two months' salary – but collective agreements may increase it and there is no legal upper limit. Collective redundancy has only recently been regulated in the Czech Republic, since the beginning of 2001. It is defined as the lay-off within 30 calendar days of at least ten workers by an enterprise with 20–100 employees, or 10 per cent of the workforce by an enterprise with 101–300 employees, or 30 workers by an enterprise with more than 300 employees. The Labour Code requires the employer to inform the trade union at least 30 days before the intended staff cut and suggest measures for its avoidance or limitation. The employer is further obliged to inform the local PES about the intended redundancies, measures for their prevention and the results of negotiations with the trade union. Notice can be given no sooner than 30 days after the submission of this information to the labour office.

Estonia, similarly to Poland, respects seniority, in terms of both the notice period and the severance pay. Where the enterprise is bankrupt or in liquidation, or staff are being cut for economic reasons, redundant workers employed with the same employer for less than five years receive at least two months' notice. The length of notice for those employed for between five years and ten years is three months, while workers with job tenure of over ten years are entitled to four months' notice. Termination justified by an inability to meet the tasks for health and qualification reasons requires only one month's notice. However, as with enterprise restructuring, the employer is required to offer another job to such workers if possible. If a vacancy is opened within six months and the laid-off worker meets its skill requirements, the employer is obliged to offer him/her this job. Reaching the age of 65 and the entitlement to a pension can also justify a dismissal; in such a case the notice period is two months for persons with service of fewer than ten years, and three months for those with ten years and more. The employer is requested to inform the trade union or any other body representing workers about the reasons for redundancy and measures to avoid it. Similar information is provided to the PES, with no other commitment for the employer. Pregnant women, youths under the age of 18 and mothers with children under three years can have their contracts terminated only with the consent of the labour inspector. Severance pay is provided to workers made redundant as a result of bankruptcy, liquidation or restructuring of the enterprise, at the level of two months' salary for those with less than five years' tenure, three months for workers with tenure of between five and ten years, and four months for those with more than ten years of service. Workers dismissed because of an inability to meet job requirements get compensation at the level of one month's salary. Estonia does not have any special procedure for collective redundancy.

In the Russian Federation, the notice period is uniform for all workers and set at two months.[5] The employer is obliged to offer another job to the redundant worker if one is available. In the case of trade union members, the trade union organization must be informed about the intended redundancy and give its consent, which is valid only for one month. Both these conditions may (and in reality often do) considerably protract employment termination and are often quoted as an important reason for choosing other ways of employment reduction, through mutual agreement or by pushing workers to quit "voluntarily" by using administrative leave, short-term work or non-payment of wages, with no obligation put on employers. Workers' groups protected against employment termination comprise pregnant women, women with children under the age of three, single parents with children under 14 years old and youths below the age of 18. They can be terminated only if their contract expires and they are offered an alternative employment, youths only with the consent of a dedicated commission for minors. Trade union officials can be dismissed only with the consent of the higher-level trade union body. Severance pay is provided at the level of two weeks' salary to workers made redundant through incapacity for reasons of health or qualifications, long-term absence (over four months), refusal to transfer to another suitable job, or military service. In the case of redundancy connected with the enterprise liquidation, bankruptcy or restructuring, the level of severance pay is equal to one month's salary. If the redundant worker does not find a new job after one month, he or she is entitled to another month's pay. After the second month of unsuccessful job search, the worker can obtain another monthly salary (again paid by the employer) under the condition that he or she registers as a jobseeker at the local labour office.

---

[5] The Russian labour legislation analysed in this section was in effect until the end of 2001. Because complete information was not available at the time of writing, new legislation effective as of January 2002 has not been included in the analysis here or in later chapters.

The Russian Federation does not have any precise definition of collective redundancy. The Employment Act obliges employers to inform the concerned employees, the trade union and the local PES about the intended mass lay-off at least three months in advance. The trade union organization assesses whether employers have properly met the employment termination procedure and, in particular, whether they have offered alternative jobs to redundant workers. Without its consent, mass redundancy cannot be implemented.

## 5.3.2 Temporary employment

In contrast with the regulation of permanent employment, there are vast differences among the five countries in EPL concerning temporary employment. None of the selected transition countries has any explicit regulation of agency work, however, as this is still rarely used.

In Bulgaria and the Russian Federation, fixed-term contracts are permitted only in special cases, specified by law. In Bulgaria, fixed-term contracts can be concluded only for (i) the replacement of a temporarily absent worker; (ii) jobs occupied on the basis of a competition, before the competition procedure is completed and the winner installed; or (iii) the period of performing a clearly specified piece of work.[6] In the Russian Federation, the conclusion of a fixed-term contract is allowed only in the case of (i) seasonal work up to six months; (ii) temporary work up to two months; (iii) substitution for a temporarily absent worker up to four months; or (iv) if the worker wishes so and it is in his or her interest. However, fixed-term contracts cannot be used for testing the ability of workers to do certain jobs, as the Labour Code forbids any assessment of performance and professional abilities during the first year of employment.

In the Czech Republic, school leavers from training facilities, secondary or tertiary schools who are taking up employment corresponding to their qualifications cannot be offered fixed-term contracts, unless these persons themselves request it in writing. In contrast, fixed-term contracts can be concluded with disabled persons.

Only Poland puts a limit on the number of renewals of fixed-term contracts: after two renewals the third renewal automatically converts the contract to a permanent one. Bulgaria limits the total period of temporary employment to three years.

Fixed-term contracts end on an agreed date. However, in Bulgaria if the worker continues his or her work for at least five days beyond the contract's end date, without a written protest by the employer, the contract automatically becomes permanent. In Estonia, the employer is obliged to give notice to the worker at least 14 days before the contract's end if it has been fixed for one year or more, or five days' notice if the

---

[6] A draft amendment to the Labour Code has been discussed in Parliament, which moderates the conditions for using fixed-term contracts. The draft amendment allows their application for any temporary work or for recruitment of workers by enterprises in financial problems or in liquidation. In addition, any enterprise can exceptionally recruit workers on fixed-term contracts of at least one year (shorter periods are permitted only upon written request by the worker) and this contract can be renewed only once (Beleva and Tzanov, 2001).

contract has been for less than one year; otherwise the contract becomes permanent. The contract is automatically terminated, however, when the worker stops work at its expiry. The notice period is not required in the case of replacement for an absent worker. In Poland the parties can agree on a notice period when concluding a fixed-term contract. In other countries the change to a permanent contract is valid when the employee continues working with the consent of the employer.

In Estonia, if the employer does not adhere to the notice period he or she is obliged to pay compensation for each working day short of the notice period. In all the countries, fixed-term contracts may be terminated before their end date either by mutual agreement or by notice with compensation, usually depending on the length of the contract. They can also be terminated without notice, either following a serious breach of rules or in the case of sickness, disability, care for family members, education or similar.

Apart from fixed-term contracts, work can also be performed under the Civil Code, which usually specifies precisely the conditions for the use of "civil contracts". In general, civil contracts are applied for seasonal work or performance of a special task and often are also strictly time-limited. As a rule, persons performing such work are not covered by occupational safety and health rules or by employer-provided social and health insurance. When the contract expires they are not entitled to unemployment benefits. Although civil contracts have been intended as agreements between independent parties on performing one-off tasks, in practice they are often applied for de facto regular employment relationships. Employers economize on overhead costs, protection measures and equipment and profit from highly flexible labour. The state budget and the social and health funds, however, lose income from taxes and social contributions.[7] The precarious position of workers under civil contracts, the use of which expanded from the start of economic transformation, and the lower level of taxes and contributions were the major reasons why several transition countries tried to stop the misuse of such contracts. In Poland, the 1996 amendment to the Labour Code changed all civil contracts which were actually covering employment relationships into regular employment contracts.[8]

The strictness of the EPL described above (for a summary, see Annex 5.1) will now be assessed using the method suggested by the OECD. To date, only ad hoc EPL indicators have been produced according to specific research needs, such as the World Bank's indicators for EU accession countries. There is a need for recognized indicators for the all transition countries.

---

[7] Individuals working on civil contracts are responsible for paying their own income tax and social contributions. However, with concessions for small entrepreneurs valid in some countries, frequent underreporting of income and over-reporting of tax-deductible costs, the actual level of income tax and social contributions paid by these individuals is considerably lower than that paid by employers and employees in the context of regular employment.

[8] Kwiatkowski, Socha and Sztanderska (2001), however, admit that this amendment could not cover all cases and certain misuse of civil contracts persists.

# 5.4 MEASURING EPL STRICTNESS

## 5.4.1 Methodology

Measuring employment protection is a difficult task, so different indicators of EPL strictness have been developed and applied. Quantitative aspects can be easily computed, such as the number of months' notice required for individual dismissal and severance pay. But other aspects, such as the interpretation of the definition of "just cause" for termination, are more difficult to measure precisely. However, these problems have been partly overcome by the positive correlation of the different indicators to each other to produce unambiguous cross-country rankings of EPL.

Table 5.1 provides rankings of the OECD-19 on the basis of several indicators measuring EPL strictness (the higher the value, the stricter the indicator of EPL). Although different methodologies obviously give varying results, the overall tendency is for countries of Southern Europe to have the strictest regulations and for these regulations to get weaker moving further north. In Europe, Switzerland, Denmark and the United Kingdom have the weakest laws protecting employment, broadly comparable with the United States in this respect.

As indicated in table 5.1, the OECD has produced EPL indicators (for both regular and fixed-term contract workers) to study the relationship between EPL and labour market outcomes for its member countries: these indicators consider a whole set of regulations that are weighted according to their importance. This methodology has been updated and enlarged to consider regulation concerning collective dismissals (OECD, 1999), and it is this version that is used here for the transition countries.

Table 5.2 presents the 22 different items describing various aspects of legislation protecting employment, covering both permanent and temporary contracts, as well as collective dismissals. These items are aggregated in three steps, from one level to the next, using a set of weights. Level 1 refers to updated (1999–2000) and detailed information collected by national experts and presented in the previous section. Some of the components can be easily quantified (for example, the length of notice period), but some others need to be transformed into quantitative terms (for example, difficulty of dismissals), using a subjective conversion scale. In level 2 several sub-indicators are obtained referring to major components of the legislation. These include procedural inconveniences, notice and severance pay for no-fault individual dismissals, and the difficulty of dismissals. Level 3 provides three groups of indicators: one describing legislation for regular contracts; one covering temporary contracts; and one capturing the collective dismissals procedures. In a final step, these three sub-indicators are aggregated in an "overall summary indicator" using different weights. The countries with very flexible employment regulation have a low overall EPL indicator (close to 0 or 1), while those with very strict legislation have a high indicator (close to 5 or 6).

Most EPL indicators are based on the *legal* constraints that apply in each country. They are hence ill suited to tracking asymmetries in the degree of enforcement of employment protection across countries and over time. There are several important

Table 5.1    Rankings of selected OECD countries by strictness of EPL, according
to different indicators

| Country | Maximum pay and OECD[1] notice period (months)[2] | | Bertola[3] | International Organization of Employers (IOE)(1–3)[4] | Average ranking based on the four preceding columns[5] |
|---|---|---|---|---|---|
| | 1993 | 1989 | 1985 | 1985 | 1985–93 |
| United States | 0.00 | 0.36[6] | 1.0 | 0.4[6] | 1 |
| New Zealand | 0.25 | 0.72[6] | 1.3[6] | 0.4[6] | 2 |
| Canada | 1.25 | 1.65[6] | 2.0[6] | 0.6[6] | 3 |
| Australia | 3.00 | 3.26[6] | 3.1[6] | 0.9[6] | 4 |
| Denmark | 4.50 | 3.25 | 2.0 | 1.0 | 5 |
| Switzerland | 5.00 | 1.75 | 3.2[6] | 0.9[6] | 6 |
| United Kingdom | 6.00 | 2.25 | 4.0 | 0.5 | 7 |
| Japan | 1.00 | 3.71[6] | 5.0 | 1.0[6] | 8 |
| Netherlands | 4.00 | 7.25 | 3.0 | 2.5 | 9 |
| Finland | 6.00 | 10.50 | 5.5[6] | 1.0 | 10 |
| Norway | 6.00 | 9.75 | 5.9[6] | 1.5 | 11 |
| Ireland | 14.00 | 2.75 | 6.0[6] | 1.5 | 12 |
| Sweden | 6.00 | 8.50 | 7.0 | 2.0 | 13 |
| France | 3.50 | 9.50 | 8.0 | 2.5 | 14 |
| Germany | 4.50 | 12.00 | 6.0 | 2.5 | 15 |
| Austria | 14.75 | 9.00 | 7.6[6] | 1.5 | 16 |
| Belgium | 8.50 | 10.50 | 9.0 | 2.5 | 17 |
| Greece | 13.25 | 11.00 | 9.1[6] | 2.5[6] | 18 |
| Portugal | 17.00 | 12.50 | 9.5[6] | 2.0 | 19 |
| Spain | 15.00 | 11.25 | 10.0[6] | 3.0 | 20 |
| Italy | 13.00 | 14.25 | 10.0 | 3.0 | 21 |

Notes: [1] The average of OECD rankings for the strictness of protection for regular and fixed-term contract workers. [2] The sum of maximum notice and severance pay, in months. [3] Bertola's ranking is based on Emerson, 1988, and the European Community's 1985 Survey of Enterprises. [4] The average of the IOE scorings of obstacles to dismissal or use of regular and fixed-term contract workers (scale from 1 to 3). [5] This "average ranking" is the rank order of a weighted average of the indicators in the preceding columns. In the weighted average, the weight of each indicator is the inverse of the coefficient estimated when that indicator is regressed on the weighted average itself. The missing values for each indicator are estimated from these regressions. Mutually consistent estimates with these properties were obtained by an iterative procedure. [6] Figures are estimates of missing values, made by regression/extrapolation, within the table: see table note 5 above.

Source: OECD, 1994a; Bertola, 1990.

Table 5.2    Employment protection index: Selection of indicators and weighting scheme

| Level 1 | | Level 2 | Level 3 | Level 4 |
|---|---|---|---|---|
| | Weighting | Weighting | Weighting | |
| Procedures 1/2<br>Delay to start a notice 1/2 | | Procedural inconveniences 1/3 | | |
| Notice period after | 9 months 1/7<br>4 years 1/7<br>20 years 1/7 | Notice and severance pay for no-fault individual dismissals 1/3 | Regular contracts 5/12 | |
| Severance pay after | 9 months 4/21<br>4 years 4/21<br>20 years 4/21 | | | |
| Definition of unfair dismissal 1/4<br>Trial period 1/4<br>Compensation 1/4<br>Reinstatement 1/4 | | Difficulty of dismissal 1/3 | | EPL overall summary indicator |
| Valid cases other than usual "objective" 1/2<br>Maximum number of successive contracts 1/4<br>Maximum cumulated duration 1/4 | | Fixed-term contracts 1/2 | Temporary contracts 5/12 | |
| Types of work for which is legal 1/2<br>Restrictions on number of renewals 1/4<br>Maximum cumulated duration 1/4 | | Temporary work agencies 1/2 | | |
| Definition of collective dismissal 1/4<br>Additional notification requirements 1/4<br>Additional delays involved 1/4<br>Other special costs to employers 1/4 | | Collective dismissals 2/12 | | |

Source: OECD, 1999, table 2.B.2.

indications that asymmetries in enforcement may be more marked than differences in regulations per se; moreover, these may play a crucial role in affecting the work of labour markets, notably the extent of job losses and the incidence of unemployment. Bertola, Boeri and Cazes (2000) point out these caveats and provide interesting evidence on the role of jurisprudence in interpreting the laws.

## 5.4.2   EPL indicators

The results of measuring EPL strictness for selected transition countries are presented in table 5.3, which also compares the average level of EPL strictness for these countries with the EU average and the OECD average. Basically, the indicators range in integer values from 1 to 6: countries with very flexible EPL have a low overall value (close to 0 or 1), and those with very strict legislation have a high value (5 to 6). Table 5.3 indicates that transition countries do not constitute a homogeneous group. When the indicators of EPL strictness in regular employment

Table 5.3   EPL indicators in selected transition countries, late 1990s[1]

| Country | Maximum pay and notice period (months)[2] | Difficulty of dismissal (summary score)[3] | Index for regular contracts (0–6)[4] | Index for regular and temporary contracts (0–6)[5] | EPL overall summary indicator (0–6)[6] |
|---|---|---|---|---|---|
| Bulgaria | 7 | 2.9 | 2.3 | 2.5 | 2.8 |
| Czech Republic | 5 | 3.2 | 3.0 | 1.8 | 2.2 |
| Estonia | 8 | 2.9 | 2.9 | 2.1 | 2.4 |
| Hungary | 8 | 2.5 | 2.1 | 1.5 | 1.8 |
| Poland | 3 | 2.7 | 2.3 | 1.7 | 2.0 |
| Russian Federation[7] | 5 | 3.5 | 3.3 | 2.9 | 3.2 |
| Slovakia | 4 | 2.4 | 2.6 | 1.9 | 2.3 |
| Slovenia | 16 | 4.5 | 3.4 | 3.0 | 3.3 |
| **Transition average[7]** | – | **3.1** | **2.7** | **2.2** | **2.5** |
| **EU average[8]** | – | – | **2.4** | **2.2** | **2.4** |
| **OECD average[9]** | – | – | **2.0** | **1.9** | **2.0** |

Notes: [1] Estimates are given for 1999, i.e. before the recent revisions of the Labour Codes of Poland, the Russian Federation and Slovenia. [2] The sum of maximum notice and severance pay (authors' calculations). [3] Covers the strictness of the legal definitions of unfair dismissal, the frequency of verdicts involving the reinstatement of the employees and the monetary compensations typically required in the case of unfair dismissals. [4] Summary score for overall strictness of protection against dismissals. [5] Weighted average of indicators for regular contracts and temporary contracts. [6] Weighted average of indicators for regular contracts, temporary contracts and collective dismissals. [7] Unweighted averages for transition, EU and OECD countries. [8] Does not include Greece and Luxembourg. [9] Selected OECD countries.

Sources: Authors' calculations; OECD, 1999; and Riboud, Silva-Jauregui and Sanchez-Paramo, 2002.

Figure 5.1 EPL index in selected OECD and transition countries, late 1990s

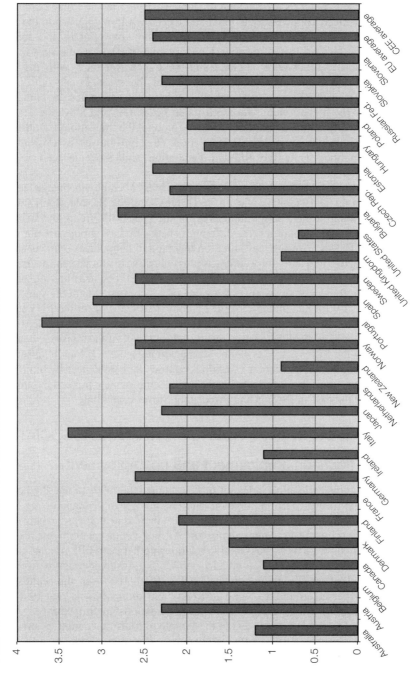

in the selected countries are compared, Hungary, Bulgaria and Poland are amongst the most flexible, followed by Estonia and the Czech Republic, while the Russian Federation is the most restrictive. If regulations on regular and temporary employment are considered together, Hungary takes the lead as the least restrictive country, closely followed by Poland and the Czech Republic, with the Russian Federation and Slovenia at the opposite end of the scale. Finally, the indicator measuring overall EPL strictness again shows the lowest values for Hungary and Poland and the highest values for the Russian Federation and Slovenia. The results prove that substantial disparities do exist among the transition countries, with Hungary having the most flexible legislation, closely followed by Poland and the Czech Republic, while the Russian Federation and Slovenia tend to be the most restrictive.

As we saw in table 5.1, differences in the strictness of employment legislation exist among the OECD-19 too (see Nickell, 1997; OECD, 1999; Bertola, Boeri and Cazes, 2000). Looking at the average indicators for the OECD-19 group, the EU and our sample of transition countries, the differences between these groups are not so great. For the indicators covering legislation on regular and temporary contracts and those covering regular and temporary contracts plus collective dismissals, the average of the selected transition countries is at the same level as the EU countries and slightly above the OECD-19 average (respectively, a value of 2.2 compared with the same level of the EU and 1.9 for the OECD-19; and 2.5 compared with 2.4 for the EU and 2.0 for the OECD-19). However, if the Russian Federation and Slovenia are excluded (and EPL has indeed been relaxed there very recently), the average of the transition countries is well below the EU average, as can be seen again in figure 5.1. Finally, it seems that when reforming their legislation, transition countries were influenced by some Western European schemes: this is reflected in the overall employment protection ranking, for example in the case of Estonia and Sweden, or Slovenia and Italy.

## 5.5  PRELIMINARY EVIDENCE (BIVARIATE ASSOCIATIONS)

### 5.5.1  Effects on employment and unemployment

Figure 5.2 plots the overall indicator of EPL in the late 1990s (along the horizontal axis) against measures of employment and unemployment averaged over 1992–98 (along the vertical axis). Figure 5.2 suggests that there is no association between EPL strictness and overall unemployment (part A), nor youth unemployment (part B). However, it shows a weak but positive relationship between EPL strictness and the overall employment-to-population ratio (part C). This result contrasts with empirical evidence based on OECD countries (OECD, 1999). However, the scatter of data points is dispersed around two opposite trends, and taking the sole year 1998 instead of the average for employment rates makes the relationship disappear.

Part D of figure 5.2 shows that in the sample of transition countries stricter EPL is not particularly associated with a higher share of self-employment, as is the case for the OECD-19, but with a lower share. However, this result should be interpreted

Figure 5.2  EPL strictness, unemployment and employment

A.  LFS unemployment rates, averages over 1992–98

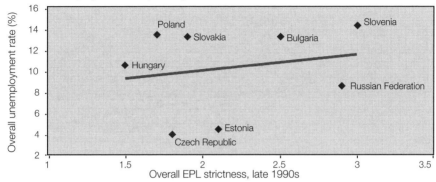

Note: Unemployment rate = 1.5*; EPL + 7.1; $R^2$ = 0.04.

B.  LFS youth unemployment rates, averages over 1992–98

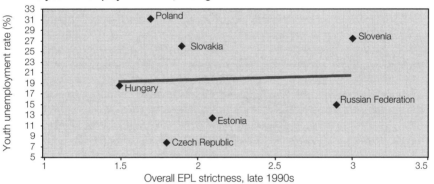

Note: Youth unemployment rate = 0.7*; EPL + 18.2; $R^2$ = 0.0023.

C.  Overall employment-to-population ratio, averages over 1994–98

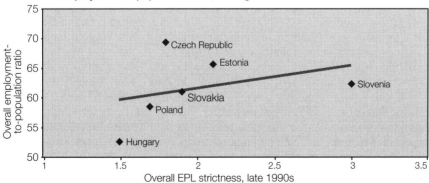

Note: Employment-to-population ratio = 3.8*; EPL + 54.0; $R^2$ = 0.117.

Figure 5.2 (cont.)   EPL strictness, unemployment and employment

D.   Shares of self-employment, 1999

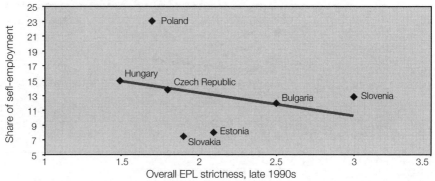

Note: Self-employment rate = −3.1*; EPL + 19.5; $R^2$ = 0.0988.

E.   Temporary employment, 1999

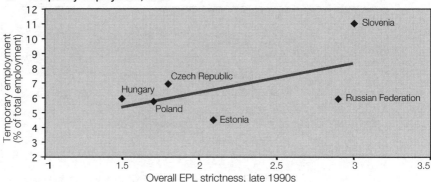

Note: Temporary employment rate = 1.98*; EPL + 2.36; $R^2$ = 0.3085.

with great caution, for several reasons. First, there are some important differences in the specification and pattern of self-employment between Western industrialized countries and transition countries (see Chapter 3); second, few observations are available (only 1999 data are considered in the analysis); and lastly, substantial differences exist among transition countries in their shares of self-employment, which makes the sample very heterogeneous. Finally, part E of figure 5.2 shows the relationship between EPL strictness and the share of temporary jobs in the selected transition countries. As mentioned before, stricter regulation of regular contracts is expected to increase the share of temporary employment, while stricter regulation of temporary contracts should reduce it, so that the overall effect of EPL is rather ambiguous. Our bivariate analysis seems to indicate a positive link between overall EPL strictness and the share of temporary employment in transition countries.

## 5.5.2   Effects on labour market dynamics

Figure 5.3 examines the bivariate association between the overall indicator of EPL stringency (again along the horizontal axis) and various measures of labour market dynamics (along the vertical axis). These scatter plots are generally consistent with theoretical predictions (see first section of this chapter), in particular when one specific sub-index of the overall indicator of EPL is considered, namely the difficulty of dismissals[9] (see table 5.3). The reason for choosing this particular indicator of the strictness of the legislation is that it is the one that bears the strongest correlation with labour market flows in the OECD countries (see Bertola, Boeri and Cazes, 2000). As stated, some associations can be found between this sub-index and labour market dynamics. In particular, figure 5.3, part A, shows that stricter EPL is rather strongly associated with lower rates of labour turnover in the selected transition countries, which is the same relationship as in the OECD-19. On the other hand, as part B of figure 5.3 indicates, stricter EPL is positively but rather weakly associated with average job tenure (once again, as in the OECD countries). This is consistent with theoretical arguments that EPL creates more employment stability and durable employment relationships. Finally, part C of figure 5.3 also suggests that stricter EPL tends to be positively but weakly associated with longer duration of unemployment. Related to this result, another relationship was also found between stricter EPL and lower flows into unemployment (not presented here); however, data were unfortunately not available to study the flows *out* of the unemployment pool.

## 5.6   CONCLUSIONS

This chapter presented the main changes in legislation protecting employment over the 1990s. It also provided new cross-country evaluations of the strictness of EPL in selected transition economies in the late 1990s, using OECD methodology. These indicators show that employment protection rules differ across transition countries, but on average at the end of the 1990s the EPL rules of the group of CEE countries were found to be as liberal as those of the EU and only slightly stricter than those of the selected OECD countries. Moreover, after the latest Labour Code amendments in Poland, Slovenia and the Russian Federation, on average legislation in the CEE countries seems to be becoming more liberal than the EU and close to the average of the OECD countries.

The impact of EPL on the labour market performance and labour market flows in transition countries seems to be rather modest. However, it is not insignificant when considering the labour reallocation processes of these countries. Labour market institutions seem to have contributed to shaping the adjustment of the labour market, such as stricter EPL lowering labour turnover. Our analysis has also revealed positive (although weak) associations of, on the one hand, stricter EPL and temporary

---

[9] This sub-index covers the strictness of the legal definitions of unfair dismissal, the frequency of verdicts involving the reinstatement of the employees and the monetary compensation typically required in the case of unfair dismissals.

Figure 5.3  EPL strictness and labour market dynamics

A.  Labour turnover, averages over 1993–98

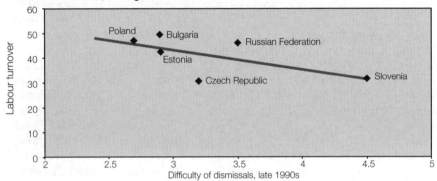

Note: Labour turnover = –7.9*; EPL + 66.8; $R^2$ = 0.4099*.

B.  Average job tenure, 1998

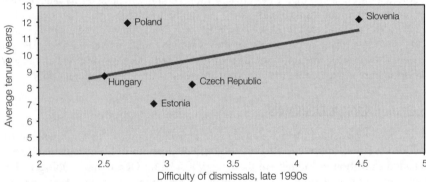

Note: Average job tenure = 1.4*; EPL + 5.22; $R^2$ = 0.2232.

C.  Long-term unemployment, averages over 1993–98

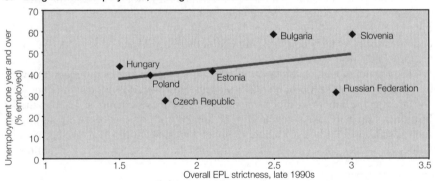

Note: Long-term unemploymet rate = 8.0*; EPL + 25.1; $R^2$ = 0.1532.

employment, and on the other hand, difficulty of dismissal and average job tenure. This would point to a certain tendency towards labour market segmentation where stronger employment protection could lead to longer job tenures of certain groups of workers, usually permanent contract holders, while increasing the incidence of temporary employment for other more vulnerable groups of workers. In the next phase of our research project we will deepen our analysis by including more countries in our survey, comparing changes in EPL in different periods and reflecting the latest legislative changes in the EPL strictness measurement.

Undoubtedly, macroeconomic and structural reforms have also significantly affected labour market adjustment in the region. In addition, the role of other labour market institutions, such as passive and active labour market policies, the power of trade unions and the tax burden on labour are all to be considered. These elements will be elaborated on in Chapter 6.

Annex 5.1  EPL in selected transition countries

| Item | Bulgaria | Czech Republic | Estonia | Poland | Russian Federation |
|---|---|---|---|---|---|
| A.  Permanent contracts | | | | | |
| *A.1 Individual dismissal* | | | | | |
| Reason for dismissal | (1) Bankruptcy or closure of enterprise or its part<br>(2) Staff reduction<br>(3) Inability to perform job due to lack of required qua ifications or abilities<br>(4) Refusal to move when job is relocated<br>(5) Change in skill requirements for a job, incompatible with worker's qualifications<br>(6) Eligibility for old-age pension but not earlier thar 2–3 years after reaching retirement age | (1) Bankruptcy or closure of enterprise or its part<br>(2) Staff reduction<br>(3) Inability to perform job due to lack of required qualifications or abilities<br>(4) Refusal to move when job is relocated | (1) Bankruptcy or closure of enterprise or its part<br>(2) Staff reduction<br>(3) Inability to perform job due to lack of required qualifications or abilities<br>(4) Age of 65 and eligibility for old-age pension | (1) Bankruptcy or closure of enterprise or its part<br>(2) Staff reduction<br>(3) Inability to perform job due to lack of required qualifications or abilities | (1) Bankruptcy or closure of enterprise or its part<br>(2) Staff reduction<br>(3) Inability to perform job due to lack of required qualifications or abilities<br>(4) Refusal to move when job is relocated<br>(5) Long-term absence due to sickness (over 4 months) |
| Notice period | 30 days<br>Possibility to agree on longer period up to 3 months | 2 months<br>If reasons (1) or (2): 3 months | For reasons (1) and (2) and length of service:<br><5 years: minimum 2 months<br>5–10 years: minimum 3 months<br>10+ years: minimum 4 months<br>For reason (3): 1 month<br>For reason (4) and length of service:<br><10 years: 2 months<br>10+ years: 3 months | Length of service:<br><6 months: 2 weeks<br>0.5–3 years: 1 month<br>3+ years: 3 months<br>In case of reasons (1) or (2) possibility to shorten to 1 month and compensate for the rest | 2 months |

| | | | | | |
|---|---|---|---|---|---|
| Procedural obligations | Notice in writing. Consent of trade unions required only in case of trade union representatives | Notice in writing. Notification to trade union and local labour office required. Consent of trade union required in case of trade union functionaries. If reasons (1) or (2) and internal redeployment impossible, employer obliged to cooperate with labour office in external re-employment of dismissed workers. If reason (3), employer obliged to warn the worker 12 months in advance | Notice in writing. If reasons (1), (2) or (3), employer obliged to redeploy the worker internally if possible. Notification to trade union and local labour office required | Notice in writing. Notification to and consent of trade union required except for bankruptcy or liquidation of enterprise | Notice in writing. Employer obliged to redeploy the worker internally if possible. Notification to and consent of trade union required (consent valid only for 1 month) |
| Restrictions | For reasons (1 – closure of part of enterprise), (2), (3) and (5): Pregnant women, mothers of children under 3 years old, persons on sickness leave, wives of conscripts and disabled persons can be dismissed only with consent of labour inspectorate | Pregnant women and persons on sickness leave protected, employer obliged to ensure re-employment of single parents caring for children aged 15 or under, disabled persons and persons no longer able to perform the job due to potential occupational disease, unless agreed otherwise | Pregnant women, mothers of children under 3 years old, young people less than 18 years old and persons on sickness leave only with consent of labour inspectorate | Pregnant women, women on maternity leave, persons on parental leave and sickness leave, persons having 2 years or less to retirement age and eligible for old-age pension, unless in case of bankruptcy or liquidation of enterprise | Pregnant women, mothers of children aged under 3 years old or disabled children less than 18 years old, single parents caring for children under 14 years old only when the employer offers them alternative employment. Youths under 18 years old only with consent of commission for minors |
| Compensation | 2 months' salary. For people employed more than 10 years with the same employer: 6 months' salary | 2 months' salary. Collective agreement or internal directive may extend it | For reasons (1), (2) and (4) and length of service: <5 years: 2 months' salary; 5–10 years: 3 months' salary; 10+ years: 4 months' salary. For reason (3): 1 month's salary | No compensation unless reasons (1) or (2) when the notice period is shortened to 1 month and salary is paid for the non-observed part | For reasons (1) or (2): up to 3 months' salary (1 month is obligatory; if the worker does not find a job, 2 more months' salary are paid but registration at labour office required for third month). For reasons (3) and (4): 2 weeks' salary |

*cont.*

*A.2 Collective dismissal*

| | | | | |
|---|---|---|---|---|
| Definition | Collective dismissal stipulated in the Employment Act without any concrete definition | Within 30 days dismissed at least: 10 employees in a firm with 20–100 employees or 10% of staff in a firm with 101–300 employees or 30+ employees in a firm with over 300 employees | Does not exist | Does not exist | Collective dismissal stipulated in the Employment Act without any concrete definition |
| Notice period | 30 days unless longer period up to 3 months agreed | At least 30 days after notification of labour office | | | At least 3 months |
| Procedural obligations | Notification to local labour office, local body for tripartite cooperation and local government 60 days in advance. If more than 150 redundancies expected, notification to national labour office | Notification to trade union at least 30 days in advance. Negotiations with trade union on measures preventing or limiting the extent of redundancies. Notification to local labour office on mass redundancy, measures undertaken and results of negotiations with trade union | | | Notification to trade union and local labour office at least 3 months in advance. Trade union assesses whether the employer has met all termination procedures and offered alternative employment. Final consent of trade unions necessary |
| Compensation | 1 month of salary; collective agreement may extend it. Alternatively: BGL1,000 instead of unemployment benefits plus additional BGL1,000 if taking up a new job or starting own business | Same as for individual dismissal | | | Same as for individual dismissal |

B. Fixed-term contracts

| | | | | | |
|---|---|---|---|---|---|
| Restriction | Only permitted in the following cases: (1) Substitution for absent workers (2) Jobs filled on the basis of competition until the position is filled (3) Completion of specific work (4) When the worker so requires | Not allowed for graduates from apprentice schools, secondary schools and universities within 2 years after completing their studies if recruited for work corresponding to their qualifications unless the person so requires | No restriction | No restriction | Only permitted in the following cases: (1) Seasonal work up to 6 months (2) Specific work up to 2 months (3) Substitution for temporarily absent workers (up to 4 months) (4) When the worker so requires |
| Maximum number of contracts | No limit | No limit | No limit | Two. Third contract becomes automatically permanent | No limit |
| Maximum cumulative length of subsequent contracts | 3 years | No limit | No limit | No limit | No limit |
| Restrictions on termination of contract | In case of early termination agreement on compensation without concrete rules. If the worker continues working for at least 5 days after the term and the employer does not protest in writing, the contract becomes permanent | Early termination upon agreement. If the worker continues working with the consent of the employer, the contract becomes permanent | Notice period 5 days for contract under 1 year, 14 days for 1+ year contract unless the contract is for substitution for absent worker. If notice period not observed, compensation provided for non-observed part | Contract longer than 6 months may be terminated with 2 weeks' notice, if not observed, eligibility for compensation by two weeks of salary | Pregnant women, mothers with children aged under 3 and disabled children under 18 years old and single parents caring for children under 14 years old can be dismissed only when the employer offers them alternative employment. Early termination compensated by two weeks of salary |

C. Agency work

| | | | | | |
|---|---|---|---|---|---|
| | No arrangement | No arrangement | No arrangement | No arrangement | No arrangement |

# THE ROLE OF LABOUR MARKET INSTITUTIONS, SOCIAL DIALOGUE AND LABOUR TAXATION

# 6

## 6.1    INTRODUCTION: BEYOND EPL

The objective of this chapter is to shed some light on the ongoing debate about the role of labour markets, institutional settings and their effect on the labour market performance of the transition countries. Labour market regulations are generally introduced to improve the employment and income security of workers through benefits and/or social security programmes. However, as benefits also induce costs, budget constraints need to be considered in policy choices: in a market economy, unemployment benefits may lead to a reduction in employment, and employment protection may protect some workers (those already in employment, with long tenure) at the expense of others (youths, the long-term unemployed and so on). The argument that the poor performance of European countries is a result of their labour market rigidities is an example of this trade-off, and it suggests that these countries' performance would be maximized by full labour market flexibility (produced by weakening trade union power and labour market regulations, for example). This proposition has strong political implications, however, since it questions both the access to employment and the quality of this employment.

While more emphasis was given in the previous chapter to the legislation protecting employment (i.e. the limitations on employers to dismiss workers at will), other forms of labour market regulations are also considered here, such as unemployment benefit systems, wage-setting institutions, active LMP (labour market) and taxes on labour. Some of these institutional schemes belong to the welfare state, as they provide income guarantees. When considered "too generous", they are accused of creating unemployment through work disincentives and wage expectations. Other labour market regulations may influence the wage structure and/or labour costs.

The "Eurosclerosis" debate (the European labour market has been said to be "sclerotic", because of the full range of labour protection schemes) has renewed relevance with the possible enlargement of the EU to the CEE countries. As the candidate countries are required to harmonize their laws and regulations with those of the EU ("*acquis communautaire*"), it is interesting to examine where the CEE countries stand in terms of labour market flexibility/rigidities. The two key issues here are, therefore, first, to assess the extent to which these accession countries – and the transition countries in general – have adopted the same labour market institutions as the EU; and second, to assess the impact, if any, of these institutions on labour market performance. In short, this chapter will try to answer the following question: do labour market institutions matter in transition countries and, if so, why?

The chapter starts with the presentation of a set of policies and labour market institutions during the 1990s for a group of nine transition countries: Bulgaria, the Czech Republic, Estonia, Hungary, Poland, the Russian Federation, Slovakia, Slovenia and Ukraine. This makes it possible to compare the labour market institutions of the transition countries with those of the OECD-19, as well as with each other. It should also be noted that this analysis is largely focused on numerical (external) flexibility, leaving aside other types of flexibility such as functional flexibility or flexibility in working hours. Moreover, it deals with enterprises and workers in the formal economy, although the strong growth of the informal economy can be interpreted as part of the process of labour market flexibilization. Based on both theoretical and empirical evidence presented for Western industrialized countries in the previous chapter, we will try to identify possible effects of labour market institutions on the labour market performance of the selected transition countries. Finally, an econometric analysis is conducted to provide some preliminary evidence on the role played by these institutions in the context of economic transition.

## 6.2  LABOUR MARKET INSTITUTIONS IN THE LATE 1990S: TRANSITION VERSUS OECD COUNTRIES

The disappointingly poor employment performance and persistently high unemployment in the transition countries may be explained by various factors, as discussed in Chapter 2, such as the ongoing macroeconomic and structural reforms. Whether or not tight labour market regulations are also to be blamed for this poor labour market performance remains a hotly debated issue in Europe. The theoretical arguments presented in Chapter 5 provide some principles on how these regulations may affect labour market outcomes; nevertheless, the relationship between the two remains mainly an empirical question. However, measuring the degree of flexibility of labour markets is a difficult task. Quantitative measures can be based on some measurable aspects, such as the level of severance pay or unemployment benefit, the percentage of persons covered by the unemployment benefit schemes or the weight of the tax burden. Other aspects are more difficult to measure, notably in the field of employment protection: for example, the willingness of labour courts to entertain law suits filed by dismissed workers or the interpretation of the notion "just cause" for termination (see Bertola, Boeri and Cazes, 2000).

Bearing in mind these limitations, it is still possible to consider a set of institutional features and compare various countries on the basis of several indicators characterizing the system. This approach builds on work done by Nickell (1997), Nickell and Layard (1999) and the OECD (1999), but goes much further, taking into account the availability of information and the specificity of the transition countries. In this section, a selected set of labour market institutions and policies in nine transition countries is described, and a comparison is made with the institutional and policy environments of the labour markets of the EU and Western OECD countries. The "institutional package" considered here refers to the following provisions: the legislation protecting employment (discussed in detail in Chapter 5); various features of the unemployment insurance schemes and active LMP; indicators of trade union strength; and the tax burden (payroll taxes). We examine and comment on each of them in the rest of the section.

## 6.2.1 Unemployment insurance systems and active LMP

The transition economies have introduced a wide range of labour market programmes, both active and passive. The aim of these policies has been to relieve tensions in the labour market and provide income support. Passive policies include unemployment insurance schemes and early retirement, while active policies encompass job mediation, labour market training, public works, job creation, subsidized employment or mobility measures, as presented in more detail below. Classical theory suggests that generous income support influences labour market outcomes in two ways: it discourages the unemployed from seeking work (by increasing their reservation wage) and reduces the "fear" of unemployment, hence increasing the upward pressure on wages from employees (via unions, for example). Empirical research on Western industrialized countries indicates that long-term benefits may generate long-term unemployment. Less generous benefits, however, may not per se stimulate active job search and higher employment, which depends, inter alia, on the overall labour market situation and demand for labour, the extent of informal employment and demand for informal labour, the wage levels offered in vacant jobs, and social welfare. In contrast, active labour policies should facilitate re-entry into the labour market.

### Unemployment insurance schemes

Over the decade, unemployment insurance systems have increasingly become less generous. This tendency can be demonstrated by the reduction of the level of benefit payments in real terms and their duration, as well as the tightening of eligibility conditions. Table 6.1 presents the main features of the unemployment insurance systems in the nine selected transition countries in the late 1990s: replacement rates (the share of income which is replaced by the unemployment benefit); the length of the benefit; and the share of benefit recipients in total registered unemployment.

Again, diversity prevails. Table 6.1 shows that initial benefit replacement rates (the ratio of initial – and therefore highest – benefits to previous earnings) in the selected transition countries ranged from 40 to 75 per cent in 1998, with the exception

Table 6.1    Characteristics of the unemployment insurance system in selected
transition countries, 1998

| Country | Benefit replacement ratio (%)[1] | Benefit as percentage of average wage (%)[2] | Benefit duration[3] | Coverage rates (%)[4] |
|---|---|---|---|---|
| Bulgaria | 60 | 32 | 6–12 months depending on age and length of employment | 24.8 |
| Czech Republic | 60 | 24 | 6 months | 48.8 |
| Estonia | 7[5] | 75 | 6 months | 59.3 |
| Hungary | 65 | 28 | 3–12 months depending on length of employment | 73.9[6] |
| Poland | 40 | 36[7] | 12 months | 23.1 |
| Russian Federation | 75 | 26[8] | 12–24 months within 36 months | 89.5 |
| Slovakia | 60 | 33 | 6–12 months depending on length of employment | 27.0 |
| Slovenia | 63 | 44 | 3–24 months depending on length of employment | 32.6 |
| Ukraine | 100 | 23 | 180–360 days within 2 years | 53.1 |

Notes: [1] Unemployment benefit replacement rate is measured by the initial benefits level divided by previous earned wage. [2] Average benefits as a percentage of gross average wage. [3] Duration of payment. [4] Percentage of unemployed receiving unemployment insurance benefits. [5] Flat rate of EEK300. [6] The ratio includes means-tested unemployment assistance, once benefits are exhausted. In contrast with other transition countries, this de facto social assistance is paid from the labour market fund, while in other countries it is usually paid from social budgets. [7] Flat rate of PLN393.60 in June 1999. [8] It broadly corresponds to 42 per cent of the national subsistence level in 1997.

Sources: O'Leary, Nesporova and Samodorov, 2001; Riboud, Silva-Jauregui and Sanchez-Paramo, 2002; communication from the national employment services.

of the two extremes: Estonia (7 per cent) and Ukraine (100 per cent). An alternative way to compare the benefit level across countries is to express the average benefit as a percentage of the average wage. Countries also differ in terms of benefit duration, ranging from six months in the Czech Republic or Estonia to 24 months in Slovenia or the Russian Federation, in line with those of the EU and the Western OECD countries (some EU countries even offer benefits of unlimited duration). Another interesting feature of unemployment insurance refers to the coverage rates of the system, that is, the percentage of registered unemployed persons receiving unemployment benefits. These rates also vary widely across countries, from 25 to 90 per cent. Moreover, the development of the rates over the decade – not shown here – was different. While they remained fairly stable in the Czech Republic, Estonia and

Table 6.2   Spending on passive and active LMP in selected transition countries, 1998

| Country | LMP expenditure as percentage of GDP[1] | | | LMP expenditure per unemployed person[2] | | |
|---|---|---|---|---|---|---|
| | Total | Passive policies | Active policies | Total | Passive policies[3] | Active policies |
| Bulgaria | 0.80 | 0.46 | 0.12 | 0.056[4] | 0.029[4] | 0.007[4] |
| Czech Republic | 0.40 | 0.26 | 0.05 | 0.055 | 0.036 | 0.007 |
| Estonia | 0.20 | 0.10 | 0.07 | 0.020 | 0.010 | 0.007 |
| Hungary | 1.30 | 0.91 | 0.28 | 0.167 | 0.117 | 0.036 |
| Poland | 1.00 | 0.59 | 0.30 | 0.095 | 0.056 | 0.028 |
| Russian Federation | 0.20 | 0.13 | 0.02 | 0.015 | 0.010 | 0.002 |
| Slovakia | 1.10 | 0.56 | 0.32 | 0.088 | 0.044 | 0.026 |
| Slovenia | 1.72 | 0.89 | 0.83 | .. | 0.110 | 0.110 |
| Ukraine | 0.30 | 0.19 | 0.03 | 0.027 | 0.017 | 0.003 |
| **EU average** | .. | .. | .. | .. | **1.16** | **0.16** |
| **OECD average** | .. | .. | .. | .. | **0.92** | **0.14** |

Notes: [1] The difference between the sum of passive and active policies and the total spending on LMP relates to the costs of running national PES. [2] Ratio of GDP spending on LMP to LFS unemployment rates. [3] Passive policies refer here to unemployment insurance. [4] Using LFS total unemployment rate from 1997. .. = not available.

Sources: O'Leary, Nesporova and Samodorov, 2001; Riboud, Silva-Jauregui and Sanchez-Paramo, 2002; communication from the national employment services.

Hungary, the coverage rates have fallen continuously in Poland and Slovakia (and to a lesser extent in Slovenia).

These differences in unemployment insurance systems are reflected in the level of spending on passive LMP, as presented in table 6.2. Despite the generally modest level of expenditures – transition countries spend less than 1 per cent of their GDP on unemployment insurance – differences are quite marked between Slovenia or Hungary (respectively spending 0.9 and 0.56 per cent of their GDP on passive programmes) and Estonia (spending less than 0.10 per cent). Generally, these figures are still lower than those of the EU countries, which devote on average 1.73 per cent of their GDP to income support for the unemployed. The same conclusions can be drawn comparing the spending per unemployed person.

## Active LMP

Most of the transition countries reviewed have adopted a package of active LMP similar to those in the OECD countries, including job mediation and counselling, vocational guidance, labour market training, employment subsidies, direct job creation, small business promotion and measures targeted at young people or disadvantaged groups (a detailed presentation of the programmes can be found in Nesporova, 1999). There are substantial differences with regard to the number of participants in and resources devoted to active LMP, as well as the distribution between different active programmes by country. Given the wide range of programmes, the scope of this cross-country comparison is limited to the spending on active LMP, and these results are also presented in table 6.2. Among the transition countries, Slovenia is the leader in expenditure on active labour market programmes, while Estonia spends ten times less. However, on average the level of expenditures on active LMP is rather low, ranging between 0.07 per cent (Estonia) and 0.83 per cent (Slovenia) of GDP. Adjusting these figures for the unemployment rate[1] confirms that transition countries do not spend large amounts on active policies: from about 0.002 per cent (the Russian Federation) to 0.11 per cent (Slovenia) of GDP for 1 per cent of the (LFS) unemployment rate in 1998. These figures are close to some OECD countries that have low expenditures on active LMP, such as the United States or Japan, but below both EU and the OECD average spending levels.[2]

## 6.2.2 Trade unions and wage bargaining

In most countries, trade unions play a major role in the collective bargaining process and are therefore likely to influence wage formation and labour costs. Even in countries where the number of unionized workers is low, as in France and Spain, collective agreements can in fact cover a large share of workers. Another relevant aspect to consider regarding unions is the extent to which they manage to coordinate their wage-setting activities together with employers' organizations. The government involvement in the negotiation process is another relevant aspect (again, as is the case in France).

Table 6.3 summarizes the key features of the trade unions in our sample of transition countries: namely, the union density, collective agreement coverage, and levels of coordination. Coordination may be distinguished from centralization, which refers to the level of bargaining (plant, firm, industry, region or country). Highly coordinated bargaining is not necessarily centralized, as in Germany or Denmark, for example. While empirical research has generated datasets on unions and employers' organizations for OECD countries (see Calmfors and Driffill, 1988; Layard, Nickell and Jackman, 1991; ILO, 1997; and Traxler and Kittel, 1997), few data are available for transition countries.

Before 1990, the industrial relations systems of the transition countries were characterized by central political and managerial control exercised by the State. During the decade, efforts were made to develop industrial relations typical of a market

---

[1] By calculating the ratio of GDP spent on active LMP to LFS unemployment rate (both in percentage terms).

[2] Indeed, there are substantial differences among OECD members: the Netherlands and Denmark are among the "high spending" OECD countries, with 0.55 and 0.34 per cent of GDP spent on active policies per unemployed person (against 0.16 and 0.14 per cent on average for the EU and the OECD respectively; see Riboud , Silva-Jauregui and Sanchez-Paramo, 2002).

Table 6.3    Trade unions and collective bargaining in selected transition countries, mid-1990s

| Country | Union density (%)[1] | Collective bargaining coverage[2] | Degree of coordination[3] |
|---|---|---|---|
| Bulgaria | 58.2 | 2 | 3 |
| Czech Republic | 42.8 | 2 | 1 |
| Estonia | 36.1 | 2 | 1.5 |
| Hungary | 60.0 | 3 | 1.5 |
| Poland | 33.8 | 3 | 1.5 |
| Russian Federation | 74.8 | 3 | 3 |
| Slovakia | 61.7 | 3 | 2 |
| Slovenia | 60.0 | 3 | 3 |
| Ukraine | 100 | 3 | 3 |
| **EU average** | **44.4** | .. | .. |
| **OECD average** | **39.6** | .. | .. |

Notes: [1] Percentage of salaried workers that belong to a trade union. [2] Collective bargaining coverage index takes a value of 1 when collective agreements cover less than 25 per cent of all salaried workers unionized or non-unionized, 2 if this number is between 26 and 69 per cent, and 3 when coverage is above 70 per cent. [3] The degree of trade union and employers' organization coordination is measured by an index that ranks from 1 (low) to 3 (high). The overall coordination is obtained as the average of workers' and employers' coordination. .. = not available.

Sources: Data on union density taken from ILO, 1997; Visser, 1990; and OECD, 1999. Collective bargaining coverage and degree of coordination taken from Riboud, Silva-Jauregui and Sanchez-Paramo, 2002, and authors' calculations based on Arro et al., 2001; Beleva and Tzanov, 2001, Kwiatkowski, Sacha and Sztanderska, 2001; Tchetvernina et al., 2001; and Večerník, 2001.

economy. CEE countries have all started to move away from a centralized wage-setting system, towards a collective bargaining system in the enterprise sector.[3] According to available data, the percentage of trade union membership ranges from about 34 per cent in Poland to over 74 per cent in the Russian Federation. Table 6.3 shows that collective bargaining coverage (i.e. the number of workers, unionized or not, who have their pay and working conditions determined by collective agreements in the enterprise sector), however, is high (over 70 per cent) in most transition countries, except in Bulgaria, the Czech Republic and Estonia. Yet, despite a relatively homogeneous cross-country picture indicating a rather high level of union membership and coverage, significant differences have emerged between the public and the private sectors, with much lower unionization of workers in the latter sector. Moreover, unions' negotiating power

---

[3] See, for example, the publications of the ILO-CEET office, Hungary, on social dialogue in CEE countries (http://www.ilo-ceet.hu).

depends very much on their ability to coordinate with employers, which is now actually rather low in most of the transition countries.[4]

OECD countries display greater diversity. Both the percentage of employees who belong to a trade union and those covered by collective agreements differ widely across countries. Trade union density ranges from less than 10 per cent in France to 82 per cent in Sweden. In the United States, less than 25 per cent of workers have their wages determined by collective agreements, while this percentage is above 70 per cent in most of the OECD countries (see Nickell and Layard, 1999, ILO, 2000). Furthermore, the degree of coordination varies across countries. The most coordinated unions/employers' organizations are those of Scandinavia and Austria, followed by continental Europe. The Anglo-Saxon countries show little coordination, despite high levels of trade union density and coverage in some cases, such as in Ireland (OECD, 1997, and Nickell, 1997). Generally, it could be said that workers in transition countries are still more unionized than in the EU or Western OECD countries, while the strength of trade unions and coordination of collective negotiations in these countries falls more or less within the average of the OECD-19.

How do trade unions affect the labour market? Unions, and more generally the industrial relations systems, play a crucial role in determining wage flexibility in response to economic shocks: according to certain characteristics and factors (such as the degree of coordination in wage bargaining, the level at which bargaining takes place, the union density and the coverage rate of collective bargaining), trade unions may influence the wage negotiation process through the setting of the minimum wage, bargaining over wage increases and the shaping of the wage structure. Coordination is a particularly important aspect of ensuring consensus in bargaining on macroeconomic objectives: wage increase negotiations may, for example, take precedence over negotiations on other issues, creating upward wage pressure and higher equilibrium unemployment (see, for example, Bertola, 1990); but unions may also set employment goals and accept wage restraint, trading wage moderation against additional employment creation (see Hartog, 1999, for example, on the importance of the social partners in the Dutch labour market success story). The three indicators presented in table 6.3 are likely to shape and partly reflect trade union policy, the key variable influencing labour market outcomes. Finally, the direct impact of the minimum wage on unemployment is not considered here, for several reasons: first, because our analysis focuses on employment flexibility (numerical flexibility), and second, because both the level of the minimum wage[5] and the percentage of workers actually earning it are still very low in most transition countries, meaning that the minimum wage does not play an important economic or social role there.[6]

---

[4] The level of coordination was quite high until the mid-1990s, paradoxically thanks to a tax-based income policy imposed by the government. When this policy, much opposed by the social partners, was eventually abolished around 1995, the coordination ability of the trade unions began to suffer.

[5] In the vast majority of transition countries, the minimum wage is set by statute or decree.

[6] In this respect, Poland may be an exception, as some recent analyses (World Bank, 2001, for example) suggest a negative impact of the minimum wage – set at around 40 per cent of the average wage – on the employment of low-skilled workers in less-developed Polish regions due to much lower wage and price levels there.

## 6.2.3  Taxes on labour

Usually, economists include payroll taxes, income taxes and consumption taxes under the heading of "taxes on labour", the argument being that the impact of taxation on the labour market operates via the wedge between the real labour cost for the employer and the real consumption wage received by the worker. Here we will focus only on payroll taxes, for two reasons: first, it can be argued that not only workers but also unemployed and inactive persons pay income and consumption taxes, and second, it is extremely difficult to construct a tax wedge based on reliable and consistent information on value-added taxes (VAT) and income taxes for all the selected transition countries.[7]

As figure 6.1 shows, payroll taxes – defined as the sum of employers' and employees' social security contributions – in transition countries are high, even by EU standards. Rates range from 33 per cent in Estonia to as high as 50 per cent in Slovakia. While these rates vary enormously across the OECD-19, they do not exceed 40 per cent: payroll taxes stretch from almost zero in Denmark to 38.8 per cent and 40.2 per cent in France and Italy respectively in the mid-1990s. In transition countries, deteriorating labour market outcomes push governments to increase the levels of public expenditures on unemployment insurance systems and active LMP. The ageing population, declining employment rates and elevated poverty levels place additional constraints on the funding of public pension schemes, health care and social welfare. At the same time, fiscal revenues fall considerably, particularly in periods of economic contraction, generating very strong pressure to maintain high payroll taxes. With respect to the negative effects of high taxation on employment and business development, some countries started to lower their payroll taxes and saw amendments and fiscal reforms taking place, though at a slow and gradual pace over the decade. Recently in Hungary, for example, employers' social contributions were cut by 2 percentage points to 31 per cent at the beginning of 2001.

## 6.2.4  A set of labour market institutions broadly similar to those of the EU

To summarize the previous sections, it could be said that by the end of the 1990s the selected transition countries had adopted a set of labour market institutions and policies that broadly resembled those in the Western OECD and EU countries. Therefore, adding the nine transition countries to the group of OECD countries does not seem to increase dramatically the diversity of the sample. In general, transition countries have opted for a rather average "institutional package": neither the most nor the least flexible model (as we saw in the previous chapter, the transition countries

---

[7] The income tax schedule is progressive in all the countries and the degree of progressiveness is important. In a number of countries, small firms in particular officially pay the minimum wage to their employees for tax reasons while paying another part of the wage under the table.

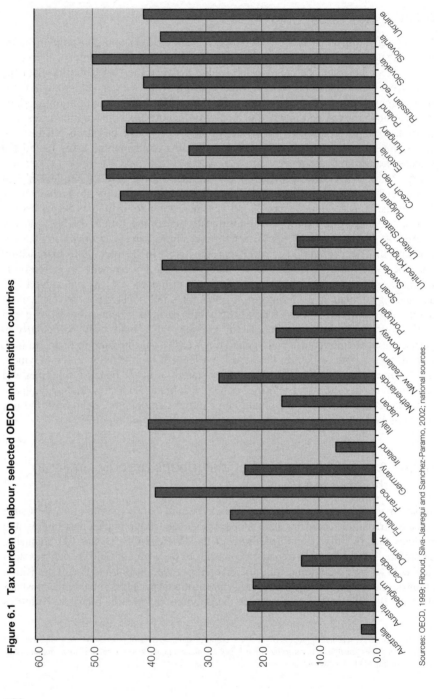

Figure 6.1  Tax burden on labour, selected OECD and transition countries

Sources: OECD, 1999; Riboud, Silva-Jauregui and Sanchez-Paramo, 2002; national sources.

are in the middle range of the flexibility scale with regard to EPL). One exception to this pattern concerns payroll taxes, which are clearly much higher (in relative terms) in the transition countries.

## 6.3 PRELIMINARY EVIDENCE IN TRANSITION COUNTRIES

### 6.3.1 Specification of the model

The main features of the labour market environment (here the independent variables) in the transition countries, as well as their potential impact on labour market outcomes, have been described in the two previous sections. The idea here is to consider theoretical and empirical evidence of the effects of labour market institutions and policies on labour market outcomes in Western industrialized countries – referring to the expected effects on job search behaviour, bargaining power, turnover, and so forth – and to test the assumption of similar responses in the transition countries.

Data on labour market institutions have been gathered for 27 countries. Two groups of countries have been considered: the OECD-19 group and eight transition countries (Bulgaria, the Czech Republic, Estonia, Hungary, Poland, the Russian Federation, Slovakia and Slovenia).[8] As it is obviously impossible to conduct an econometric analysis on the group of only eight transition countries, the hypothesis tested statistically is that the labour markets of the two groups of countries have similar behaviour vis-à-vis labour market environments. The Chow test statistic is used, which allows for a comparison of the stability of the coefficients for the two groups of data (see Annex 6.2). Therefore, a single pooled equation is first estimated on all 27 countries (OECD plus transition), then again for the OECD-19, and the Chow test statistic computed to test the similarity hypothesis.

Simple cross-country regressions are then conducted to address various aspects of unemployment (total unemployment, long-term and youth unemployment rates)[9] and aggregate labour input (employment rates and labour force participation rates). A two-year average is used in order to smooth out the cycle and year-to-year noise (1996 and 1998); ideally, an average for a longer period should be considered, but our empirical exercise is hampered by the lack of data.[10] Most of the independent variables have been presented in the previous sections and come mainly from OECD or national sources (the latter for transition countries). Because the labour market environment influences the equilibrium unemployment rates, while the actual unemployment rates are used as the dependent variables, an output gap is included.[11] This is the deviation of output from

---

[8] We could not include Ukraine in the regressions, as some data were missing.

[9] Owing to time and data constraints, we could not make estimations for the unskilled unemployment rate. In the future, however, we are planning to extend our research to other dependent variables, such as unskilled unemployment rates and prime-age employment rates, as well as flows variables.

[10] For example, most of the data come from LFS which have been launched only recently in some of the transition countries (see p. 53).

[11] Another option – although not appropriate for the transition countries – is to use the rate of change of inflation to capture this difference (for example, Nickell and Layard, 1999).

a trend generated by the Hodrick–Prescott filter (see Annex 6.1 for a detailed presentation of the data and sources).

The unemployment equation uses the log of unemployment as the dependent variable, in line with the previous theoretical and empirical research (see Nickell, 1987, and Blanchflower and Oswald, 1994). For the long-term and youth unemployment rates, the choice of the econometric specification between levels, log or semi-logarithmic is less clear (see for example Mincer, 1976; Bazen and Martin, 1991; and Esping-Andersen, 2000). Different specifications have therefore been estimated.

## 6.3.2 Summary regressions explaining labour market outcomes

### Unemployment

Table 6.4 presents the results of two different estimations of the overall unemployment rate. As this study is focused on transition countries, the results are analysed in more detail for them, while the OECD-19 are used mainly as a reference. The assumption that there is no behavioural difference between the OECD-19 and our sample of transition countries is first tested. The first column of data in table 6.4 reports a basic specification that includes the variables of the labour market "institutional package" (EPL, unemployment benefit replacement rates, duration of unemployment benefit, active LMP, union density, collective bargaining coverage, union coordination and labour taxes). A second version of this specification, which considers only the statistically significant variables, is then presented in the second column of data for, respectively, the whole sample of countries and for the group of OECD countries only. In general, the coefficient value and significance of the variables have increased in this second version.

Table 6.4 suggests that the institutional variables that seem to have an impact on the overall unemployment rates are active LMP, collective bargaining coverage and labour tax (at 10 per cent and 20 per cent levels respectively). Yet the overall effect of the trade unions is statistically ambiguous. The regression coefficients of both the union density and collective bargaining coverage variables are positive, suggesting that powerful trade unions are inversely associated with a decrease in unemployment, in line with theoretical expectations; however, these variables are not statistically significant in the first specification, and good coordination between unions and employers' organizations could offset the previous effect (with a coefficient of –0.22 for the union coordination variable). The various schemes of LMP also have different effects, although neither the replacement ratio provided by the unemployment benefit system nor the length of time for which the benefit is payable are significant. This may be explained by the presence of transition countries in the sample, which clearly exhibit less generous unemployment insurance schemes, notably regarding the duration of the benefits. The active LMP variable is statistically significant (at the 10 per cent level), which suggests that expansion of active labour market programmes may contribute to

Table 6.4  Regressions explaining the log unemployment rate (dependent variable) for selected transition and OECD countries, late 1990s

| Independent variables | Log unemployment rate (dependent variable) | | |
|---|---|---|---|
| | OECD-19 and CEE[1] (all independent variables) | OECD-19 and CEE (only statistically significant independent variables) | OECD-19 (only statistically significant independent variables) |
| Employment protection | 0.06 (0.43) | .. | .. |
| Replacement rate | 0.00 (0.36) | .. | .. |
| Benefit duration | 0.02 (0.47) | .. | .. |
| Active LMP[2] | −0.02 (−1.41) | −0.02 (−1.98) | −0.02 (−2.01) |
| Union density | 0.00 (1.08) | .. | .. |
| Collective bargaining coverage | 0.15 (1.08) | 0.18 (1.59) | 0.17 (1.30) |
| Union coordination | −0.22 (−1.40) | .. | .. |
| Labour tax | 0.01 (1.51) | 0.01 (1.59) | 0.01 (1.49) |
| Output gap | −0.11 (−2.36) | −0.10 (−2.33) | −0.23 (−2.57) |
| *Adj. $R^2$* | *0.58* | *0.50* | *0.60* |
| *Number of countries* | *27* | *27* | *19* |
| *Chow test (Fisher)* | *..* | *0.90\*\** | *..* |

Notes: Estimation is by Ordinary Least Squares (OLS). t-statistics are presented in parentheses. For the Fisher statistic, \*\* means that the hypothesis of coefficients stability is accepted at the 5 per cent level; see Annex 6.2 for more details on the Chow test.

[1] The sample of transition countries is made up of Bulgaria, the Czech Republic, Estonia, Hungary, Poland, the Russian Federation, Slovakia and Slovenia. [2] The variable measures the ratio of GDP spending on active LMP to the unemployment rate, both in percentage terms. For use in the equations, the variable is instrumented. Because the active LMP variable refers to the percentage of GDP normalized on current unemployment, it is highly endogenous. So the current percentage of GDP spent on active labour market measures is renormalized on the average unemployment rate in 1993–94 to create the instrument. In so far as measurement errors in unemployment are serially uncorrelated, this will help with the problem of endogenous variables. .. = not applicable.

reducing the level of overall unemployment (with a coefficient of –0.02). On the other hand, the estimated coefficient for the tax burden on labour (i.e. payroll taxes, in our analysis) is positive but low (0.01) and weakly significant (at 20 per cent), suggesting that higher payroll taxes may slightly increase the level of unemployment.

Finally, the coefficient for overall EPL strictness is very small and statistically insignificant, in line with previous evidence presented for OECD countries, and with the simple bivariate analysis plotting the EPL indicator against the unemployment rate (see Chapter 5). Comparing the two last columns of table 6.4, it is interesting to

Table 6.5  Regressions explaining log long-term unemployment rate (dependent variable) for selected transition and OECD countries, late 1990s

| Independent variables | Log unemployment rate (dependent variable) | | |
|---|---|---|---|
| | OECD-19 and CEE (all independent variables) | OECD-19 and CEE (only statistically significant independent variables) | OECD-19 (only statistically significant independent variables) |
| Employment protection | 0.32 (1.02) | .. | .. |
| Replacement rate | 0.00 (0.18) | .. | .. |
| Benefit duration | 0.12 (1.03) | 0.12 (1.32) | 0.14 (1.40) |
| Active LMP[1] | −0.03 (−1.01) | −0.04 (−1.54) | −0.04 (−1.42) |
| Union density | 0.01 (0.66) | .. | .. |
| Collective bargaining coverage | 0.61 (2.03) | 0.75 (3.02) | 0.93 (3.21) |
| Union coordination | −0.39 (−1.09) | .. | .. |
| Labour tax | 0.02 (1.20) | 0.02 (1.95) | 0.02 (1.18) |
| Output gap | 0.04 (0.38) | .. | .. |
| *Adj. $R^2$* | *0.57* | *0.53* | *0.58* |
| *Number of countries* | *27* | *27* | *19* |
| *Chow test (Fisher)* | *..* | *0.75\*\** | *..* |

Notes: For variables and definitions, see table 6.4. [1] See note 2, table 6.4. .. = not applicable.

note that the estimated coefficients are almost identical for the two samples, OECD plus transition countries and OECD countries only.

Turning to the long-term unemployment rates,[12] the same results are generally obtained as for the overall unemployment rates (table 6.5). First, the hypothesis of stability of the coefficients is also accepted. Second, no evidence was found that EPL was influencing the duration of unemployment, contrary to preliminary evidence based on bivariate analysis (see Chapter 5) and to the evidence found for OECD countries (a multivariate analysis conducted by the OECD, 1999, showed a

---

[12] Several modal specifications have been tested to estimate the long-term unemployment (log and level): with an output gap (not significant) and with different indicators of employment protection strictness as independent variables. The regression coefficient of the active LMP variable is statistically significant in other specifications tested, in particular when the payroll tax variable is omitted and the employment protection variable is introduced. As already stated, employment protection is not significant in the log of specification. However, this finding does not appear robust to the level specification (in conformity with the results in Chapter 5), in which stricter protection (both indicators of EPL, considering regular and temporary employment and collective dismissals) increases the level of long-term unemployment.

positive correlation between EPL strictness and the duration of unemployment). More generally, collective bargaining coverage and the payroll tax variables seem to have an impact on long-term unemployment, in the sense that it would tend to rise with an increase in these variables. This finding confirms that the primary focus of collective bargaining has so far been on the employment protection of workers covered and on the negotiation of wage increases, which leaves aside jobless persons and contributes to longer duration of unemployment. This suggests the need for an extension of social dialogue to include policies promoting employment and combating unemployment. The regression coefficient of the duration of the unemployment benefit is also positive but not significant (in line with theoretical evidence). Here again, active LMP may partly offset the previous effects by reducing the level of long-term unemployment (but the variable is weakly significant). The comparison of the regressions conducted for the two samples of countries suggests that the lack of statistical significance of the unemployment insurance variables is probably due to the presence of the transition countries, since the results for solely the OECD-19 show stronger coefficients for the replacement ratio variable (see also Scarpetta, 1996).

As discussed before, labour market institutions and policies may also affect youth unemployment rates. Table 6.6 presents two specifications. The first column of data reports the basic specification that includes all labour market institutional elements reviewed in this study, allowing for a comparison of the situation of youth in the labour market vis-à-vis overall unemployment (see the first column of data in table 6.4); the second specification concentrates on the statistically significant variables, shown in the last two columns. Here again, the assumption that there is no behavioural difference between our samples of OECD countries and transition countries has been tested and accepted on the basis of the Chow test.

Generally, the same set of variables explains youth unemployment rates and overall unemployment rates, with the exception of the trade unions, which seem to have no impact at all on youth unemployment rates: none of the regression coefficients for the three "union variables" is statistically significant, even at a low level. Moreover, the duration of unemployment benefit presents a significant statistical association with youth unemployment, in the sense that longer duration tends to increase it (with a coefficient of 0.11). In the same vein, the labour tax variable is highly significant, as shown in table 6.6, and tends to increase youth unemployment rates. Active labour market programmes, by contrast, tend to reduce it (see the second column of data in table 6.6). The main puzzling result concerns the influence of the output gap variable, which seems to be positively associated with youth unemployment rates (and negatively with overall unemployment). This result is a priori unexpected and may be explained by different factors. The first possible explanation is that the estimated specification is not the appropriate one, and some variables may be missing. Indicators for minimum wages or job shortages, for example, are variables usually considered in standard regressions of youth unemployment. These omissions could be captured by the output gap variable (see, for example, Bruno and Cazes, 1998). Another explanation may be that if employers

Table 6.6    Regressions explaining log youth unemployment rates  (dependent
            variable) for selected transition and OECD countries, late 1990s

| Independent variables | Youth unemployment rate (dependent variable) | | |
|---|---|---|---|
| | OECD-19 and CEE (all independent variables) | OECD-19 and CEE (only statistically significant independent variables) | OECD-19 (only statistically significant independent variables) |
| Employment protection | 0.22 (1.38) | .. | .. |
| Replacement rate | 0.00 (–0.25) | .. | .. |
| Benefit duration | 0.12 (1.94) | 0.11 (2.28) | 0.13 (3.11) |
| Active LMP[1] | –0.02 (–1.56) | –0.02 (–2.02) | –0.04 (–3.69) |
| Union density | 0.01 (1.07) | .. | .. |
| Collective bargaining coverage | –0.02 (–0.15) | .. | .. |
| Union coordination | –0.19 (–1.05) | .. | .. |
| Labour tax | 0.01 (2.0) | 0.02 (3.60) | 0.03 (4.90) |
| Output gap | 0.10 (1.80) | 0.10 (2.17) | 0.15 (2.56) |
| *Adj. R²* | *0.62* | *0.56* | *0.72* |
| *Number of countries* | *26* | *26* | *19* |
| *Chow test (Fisher)* | *..* | *2.01\*\** | *..* |

Notes: For variables and definitions, see table 6.4. [1] See note 2, table 6.4. .. = not applicable.

produce far below their potential, they do not need to increase their inputs (hiring new workers, in particular young inexperienced ones) to better use their capacity. Moreover, they may adjust by laying off workers, starting with the young ones (last in, first out). Finally, looking at rigidities, there is no evidence that employment protection influences youth unemployment, although a weak positive link may be found if the level specification is tested.[13] This result is also consistent with bivariate analysis that finds no effect of EPL on youth unemployment in transition countries over the last decade (see Chapter 5).

---

[13] As with long-term unemployment, several specifications have been tested to estimate the youth unemployment rate (log and level) with an output gap and with different indicators of employment protection strictness as independent variables. EPL is not significant in the log specification; however, this finding does not appear robust to the level specification in which stricter protection (both indicators of EPL, considering regular and temporary employment and collective dismissals) increases the level of youth unemployment. This result applies to the transition countries, as we accepted the hypothesis of stability of the coefficients on the basis of the Chow test.

## Labour input

Table 6.7 presents the results of the regressions addressing two labour input measures, the employment rate (employment-to-population ratio) and the labour force participation rate. As explained before, the impact of labour market institutions on unemployment or labour input arises from the theoretical mechanisms described above. However, it should be noted that other variables may contribute to explaining variations across countries in labour input, such as early retirement, disability benefits and some factors influencing the participation of women, which have not been taken into account. Therefore, the labour input equations will tend to contain more unexplained noise.

First of all, the same set of variables appears to influence significantly both employment and labour force participation rates, that is, the collective bargaining coverage and coordination variables, EPL and active LMP. Employment protection is statistically significant (at the 10 per cent level), which was not the case for equations explaining the unemployment rate. It appears to reduce both the employment rates and the labour force participation rates. This effect seems to be partly counterbalanced by active LMP. The overall effect of the trade unions is again ambiguous. The regression coefficient of the collective bargaining coverage variable is statistically significant and negative, suggesting that wide coverage tends to reduce labour supply; but again, this impact can be partly counterbalanced if unions and employers' organizations coordinate their collective bargaining activities. Finally, payroll taxes and unemployment benefits seem to have no statistical effect[14] either on employment rates or on labour force participation rates.

The results presented seem to be mostly driven by the group of OECD countries, however. If the transition countries are excluded from the sample, stronger relationships can be found between EPL or collective bargaining institutions and employment and labour force participation rates (see table 6.7). Moreover, the active LMP variable is no longer statistically significant. This is indeed confirmed by the straightforward conclusions of the statistical test on the behavioural difference between OECD and transition countries: it rejects the hypothesis of stable coefficients for the labour force participation rate, but accepts it for the employment rate, the statistic for testing this latter stability being very close to the threshold of acceptance.

The previous findings suggest that the patterns characterizing labour supply in transition countries differ from those in Western industrialized countries. As it is obviously not possible to present the results of an econometric analysis solely based on the group of transition countries, we calculated and compared the correlation coefficients between EPL and labour force participation for both groups of countries: they systematically have the opposite sign, EPL being positively correlated with labour force participation in transition countries (+0.3), while it is negative for OECD

---

[14] This is in line with evidence on OECD countries, where it is generally the overall tax burden on labour (i.e. the tax wedge) that has a clear negative impact on employment rates (see, for example, Nickell, 1997, and Nickell and Layard, 1999).

Table 6.7   Regressions explaining labour input measures (dependent variable) for selected transition and OECD countries, late 1990s

| Independent variables | Labour input measures (dependent variable) | | | |
|---|---|---|---|---|
| | Employment rate[1] | | Labour force participation rate | |
| | OECD-19 and CEE (only statistically significant independent variables) | OECD-19 (only statistically significant independent variables) | OECD-19 and CEE (only statistically significant independent variables) | OECD-19 (only statistically significant independent variables) |
| Employment protection | −2.93 (−1.74) | −3.71 (−2.11) | −2.87 (−1.97) | −3.41 (−2.54) |
| Replacement rate | .. | .. | .. | .. |
| Benefit duration | .. | .. | .. | .. |
| Active LMP[2] | 0.52 (3.18) | 0.19 (0.90) | 0.26 (1.70) | 0.12 (0.75) |
| Union density | .. | .. | .. | .. |
| Collective bargaining coverage | −5.91 (−3.17) | −6.17 (−2.93) | −3.92 (−2.28) | −4.18 (−2.60) |
| Union coordination | 2.27 (1.29) | 5.61 (2.61) | 2.69 (1.69) | 4.72 (2.87 |
| Labour tax | .. | .. | .. | .. |
| Output gap | −0.87 (−1.40) | .. | −0.39 (−0.86) | .. |
| *Adj. R[2]* | *0.63* | *0.69* | *0.57* | *0.70* |
| *Number of countries* | *27* | *19* | *27* | *19* |
| *Chow test (Fisher)* | *2.77\*\** | *..* | *3.20* | *..* |

Notes: For variables and definitions, see table 6.4. [1] Employment–to-population ratio. [2] See note 2, table 6.4.
.. = not applicable.

countries (around −0.5).[15] This confirms that our results for employment rates in the total sample are mainly driven by the sample of OECD countries, and should be used and interpreted with great caution for the transition countries. Finally, the stability of the regression coefficients was tested and rejected for labour force participation rates, consistent with our previous findings (see Chapter 4). One of our key findings is the tendency towards a countercyclical pattern of labour turnover coupled with a

---

[15] This result is also consistent with evidence based on bivariate analysis showing a weak but positive association between EPL and employment-to-population ratio (see Chapter 5). However, the results there also reveal the opposite relationship for prime-age men. Therefore a more detailed analysis (by sex and by age) would be necessary to bring about clearer trends and results.

pro-cyclical pattern of job tenure, which is the opposite of what happens in the Western industrialized countries. In Chapter 4, these differences are explained by the fact that labour reallocation in the transition countries has generally been driven more by the demand side (employers) than by workers' voluntary decisions, because of workers' heightened perception of job insecurity. Our results for labour force participation rates seem indeed to confirm this hypothesis.

## 6.3.3  Summary of the results

Generally, the hypothesis of non-stability of the coefficients of the two different groups of countries, the 19 Western OECD countries and the eight transition countries, was rejected. In other words, it can be said that the labour markets of these two groups of countries follow the same pattern in their adjustment (reaction) to the institutional setting of the labour market, using a Chow test at the 5 per cent confidence level. This finding seems particularly robust for unemployment variables. Labour force participation rates, on the other hand, have to be explained by another set of variables. Moreover, they seem to be affected by the institutional setting in an opposite way to Western industrialized countries. These results should of course be interpreted with caution. As noted, the scope of this analysis is restricted to the formal economy only. The institutional environment is also becoming more complex (non-standard forms of employment have increased, for example). Finally, indicators are far from perfect. For example, EPL indicators do not address exemptions from the application of EPL in small enterprises or the enforcement procedures (existing indicators are based on the legal constraints that apply in each country and do not capture the degree of enforcement of the laws).

## 6.4  CONCLUSIONS

This chapter analysed the main labour market institutional settings of a group of nine transition countries and showed that these countries have adopted models broadly similar to those in the EU (this is true of the CEE countries in particular). The main difference (in relative levels) refers to labour taxation, where transition countries rank among the highest. It was also found that, once again, diversity prevails within the group of transition countries.

Based on theoretical and empirical evidence for Western OECD countries, an econometric analysis was conducted to assess the potential effects of labour market institutional settings on labour market outcomes. Generally, no statistical impact of EPL was found on the various unemployment rates of transition countries. By contrast, EPL seems to influence labour supply significantly, in the sense that stricter employment protection tends to have a negative effect on employment and labour market participation rates. However, we have found that in transition countries this effect is actually opposite to that of the Western OECD countries, and that in the former group of countries more protection leads to higher levels of employment and labour market participation. The key labour market institutions on which policies of transition countries should be focused to improve their labour market situation are collective bargaining institutions and active labour market programmes. Moreover, according to our findings, payroll taxes are positively correlated with unemployment rates, in particular long-term and youth unemployment rates. This suggests that transition countries willing to cut currently high (long-term) unemployment rates may envisage gradually reducing extensive payroll taxes.

Policies promoting social dialogue, but extending it to pay greater attention to employment promotion and unemployment reduction and to ensure increased labour market stability, rather than pure deregulation, should clearly be on the political agenda of the transition countries. Reforming labour legislation should also be considered, in some countries more urgently than in others. However, this should be done while considering and combining the complete labour market institutional setting, to find the right balance between the need for flexibility (desired by employers) and security (desired by workers). Finally, it should be noted that this analysis is strongly focused on aggregate labour market outcomes, such as unemployment and labour input. It is very important that further research be developed on the adjustment of labour markets (labour market dynamics) to the macroeconomic and structural reforms that have taken place in these countries, as there have been many changes in this respect over the last decade.

# ANNEX 6.1   DEFINITIONS AND
# DATA SOURCES

Data have been gathered for 27 countries. Two groups of countries are considered: 19 OECD countries and eight transition countries. The OECD sample is made up of Australia, Austria, Belgium, Canada, Denmark, Finland, France, Germany, Ireland, Italy, Japan, the Netherlands, New Zealand, Norway, Portugal, Spain, Sweden, the United Kingdom and the United States. The transition sample is Bulgaria, the Czech Republic, Estonia, Hungary, Poland, the Russian Federation, Slovakia and Slovenia.

## Dependent variables

For the OECD countries, unemployment rates, labour force participation rates and employment rates are obtained from the OECD (2001). For the transition countries, unemployment rates, labour force participation rates and employment rates are obtained from national LFS and from the OECD (1999). Youth unemployment rates are from Eurostat (2001); data are available for all countries except the Russian Federation.

## Independent variables (labour market institutional settings)
### Trade union and collective bargaining process

(a) The union density variable is measured as the percentage of all salaried workers who belong to a trade union.

(b) The collective bargaining coverage index takes a value of 1 when collective agreements cover less than 25 per cent of all salaried workers, 2 if this number is between 26 and 69 per cent and 3 when coverage is above 70 per cent.

(c) The degree of union and employer coordination is measured by an index that ranks from 1 (low) to 3 (high). The overall coordination is obtained as the average of union and employer coordination.

Union density, collective bargaining coverage index and coordination of collective bargaining are obtained from authors' calculations, ILO (1997) and Riboud, Silva-Jauregui and Sanchez-Paramo (2002).

## Unemployment benefit schemes

(a) The unemployment benefit replacement rate is measured by the average benefits as a percentage of the average wage. An alternative measure where the average benefits are replaced by the initial benefits has also been tested in the equations. Data on replacement rates are obtained from authors' calculations.

(b) Unemployment benefit duration corresponds to the maximum duration of unemployment benefits in months. For the purpose of the estimations, the variable is converted into years with no limit substituted by a value of six years. Data on unemployment benefit duration are obtained from Riboud, Silva-Jauregui and Sanchez-Paramo (2002) and from O'Leary, Nesporova and Samodorov (2001).

## Employment protection legislation

The EPL index measures the degree of strictness of the legislation and is calculated as a weighted average of indicators for regular contracts, temporary contracts and collective dismissals (see Annex 6.2). A restricted version, which considers exclusively legislation on permanent and temporary employment, has also been tested in the equations. Data are from authors' calculations and from Riboud, Silva-Jauregui and Sanchez-Paramo (2002).

## Active labour market policies

The variable measures the ratio of GDP spending on active LMP to unemployment rate, both in percentage terms. For use in the equations, the variable is instrumented. Because the active LMP variable refers to the percentage of GDP normalized on current unemployment, it is highly endogenous. So the current percentage of GDP spent on active labour market measures is renormalized on the average unemployment rate in 1993–94 to create the instrument. In so far as measurement errors in unemployment are serially uncorrelated, this will help with the endogeneity problem. Data are obtained from the OECD (1999) and from O'Leary, Nesporova and Samodorov (2001).

## Tax burden on labour

The tax burden on labour is measured by the payroll tax rate variable. Data are from the International Social Security Association (ISSA) and Riboud , Silva-Jauregui and Sanchez-Paramo (2002).

## Output gap

The output gap is measured as the fraction of real GDP to potential GDP minus 1. It covers the same period as the dependent variables. Data for GDP at 1995 constant prices in US dollars are obtained from the World Development Indicators of the World Bank. Potential GDP is obtained from a Hodrick–Prescott filter applied to real GDP with the value of the parameter lambda set to 25.

# ANNEX 6.2  TEST METHODOLOGY

To test whether OECD and transition countries behave similarly, the Chow test statistic is used. This statistic allows us to compare coefficients of regressions calculated on two groups of data. In order to compute the test statistic, a single pooled equation is first estimated on all countries (OECD plus transition countries). Then the same model is estimated on the samples of OECD countries and transition countries separately.

Let's suppose that for both groups the pooled equation is:

$$y = a + b\,x_1 + c\,x_2 + u$$

and that we get the two following equations when we estimate that model on each group:

$$y = a_1 + b_1\,x_1 + c_1\,x_2 + u \quad \text{(for OECD countries)}$$

$$y = a_2 + b_2\,x_1 + c_2\,x_2 + u \quad \text{(for transition countries)}$$

In the pooled equation, we are asserting that $a_1 = a_2$, $b_1 = b_2$ and $c_1 = c_2$. The formula for the Chow test of this constraint is:

$$SST - (SS1 + SS2) \,/\, K \,/\, SS1 + SS2 \,/\, N1 + N2 - 2*K$$

where $SS1$ and $SS2$ are the error sums of squares from the separate regressions, $SST$ is the error sum of squares from the pooled regression, $K$ is the number of estimated parameters ($K = 3$ in our case) and $N1$ and $N2$ are the number of observations in the two groups.

The resulting test statistic is distributed as a Fisher with $K$, $N1 + N2 - 2*K$ degrees of freedom.

# POLICY CONCLUSIONS

# 7

## 7.1 A SUMMARY OF FINDINGS

The empirical analysis of the labour markets of the CEECA countries conducted in this book has shown that these markets have undergone profound changes since the beginning of their transition to a market system. While the intention was to direct labour market developments in these countries towards the situation common in the industrialized world by modelling the transformation of national labour market institutions and policies on similar, mostly Western European, institutions and policies, the outcomes have been to a large extent different from the expectations. Our findings can be summarized in ten points, as follows.

1. It has been noted that, after a sharp initial decrease, employment has not recovered greatly even in those countries embarking initially on a relatively high economic growth path. Unemployment has remained persistently high as many workers, discouraged in seeking a job, have withdrawn from the labour market altogether. Participation rates, which had once been among the highest in the world, thus declined to levels below the OECD average. This was mainly as a result of the fall in male participation rates, as those for women have still remained above the average in most of these countries.

2. In more advanced transition countries, employment structure by economic sector has followed general development trends; that is to say, declining proportions of agriculture and industry in total employment have been compensated by an increase in the share of services. However, less economically successful transition countries have experienced much deeper de-industrialization, with a simultaneous stagnation or even an increase in the share of agriculture in employment, while the contribution of services has also grown. For these countries, agriculture and partly also services have become a buffer for industrial unemployment.

3. In contrast with expectations, the numbers of employers and the self-employed performing own-account activities as their primary job have remained limited and do not contribute much to total employment.

4. There has been an upsurge in flexible forms of employment, but this has mainly been in the form of multiple-job holding or second jobs, both formal and informal, performed beside primary employment, registered unemployment or formal inactivity. The frequency of temporary employment has also risen significantly, but more in the form of civil contracts rather than fixed-term or short-term contracts regulated by the Labour Code.

5. Labour market flexibility measured by labour turnover has intensified while job stability reflected in average job tenure has declined considerably in the transition countries in the 1990s. Our analysis of correlations of labour turnover and average job tenure with the business cycle has found a countercyclical movement of labour turnover and a pro-cyclical movement of job tenure, in direct contrast to developments in the OECD countries. We explain this opposite tendency by high job, employment and income insecurity perceived by workers in transition countries, contrasting with much higher confidence in the labour market and in assistance provided by labour market and social welfare institutions enjoyed by their colleagues in industrialized countries. In consequence, in the latter group of countries in periods of economic boom people quit their old jobs more frequently to move to better jobs. High labour demand also absorbs greater numbers of unemployed persons and newcomers, while in periods of economic recession labour moves decline. Conversely, in transition countries, fear of the fragile economic situation of many companies, weak protection of workers' rights and substantial income loss when falling into unemployment cause workers to feel reluctant about quitting their jobs and moving to new ones even during economic upswings, while during economic downswings labour flows increase as many people lose their jobs or are pushed to quit "voluntarily". This finding has also been supported by a strong correlation between the economic cycle and moves from employment to unemployment or inactivity for the majority of the transition countries studied.

6. Comparisons of the strictness of EPL in the group of selected transition countries with the EU and the selected OECD countries, using the same (OECD) methodology, show that on average EPL in the CEE transition countries is similar to the EU average and slightly above the OECD average, though there are significant differences among the countries of the CEE sample. Moreover, recent changes in national labour legislation in Poland, the Russian Federation and Slovenia seem to have further moved the group of transition countries even below the OECD average.

7. While the impact of EPL on employment and unemployment has in general been found rather modest in the light of the results of our bivariate analysis, stricter EPL tends to contribute significantly towards lower labour turnover. Moreover, there seems to be a positive link between stricter employment protection on the one hand and higher temporary employment and longer average job tenure on the other, pointing to a certain labour market segmentation between "insiders" and "outsiders": the former enjoying more job stability and the latter being more exposed to precarious jobs.

8. Transition countries have adopted similar labour market institutions and policies, such as collective bargaining systems, labour taxation, unemployment benefit schemes and active LMP as their counterparts grouped in the OECD. Despite analogous schemes, there are considerable differences in the level of their application among these countries and in comparison with the Western OECD average. The degree of unionization of the workforce is still considerably higher in transition countries than in the selected OECD countries, but the trade union movement is rather fragmented in a number of countries and therefore collective negotiations play a less important role than could be the case. Within the group of transition countries, the role of trade unions seems to be higher still in the CIS countries. Labour taxation as a percentage of wages is very high in transition countries. In contrast, the level of unemployment benefits, the coverage of unemployed persons by income support and active LMP and the share of GDP devoted to LMP are generally low in all the transition countries, but particularly so in the CIS countries.

9. Our multivariate analysis has confirmed the results of the bivariate analysis, finding no statistically significant impact of EPL on the aggregate, long-term and youth unemployment rates in transition countries. However, it has identified significant correlation between the level of employment protection on the one hand and the employment and the labour market participation rates on the other, but with opposite signs for the two groups of countries. While in the Western OECD countries stricter employment protection tends to have a negative effect on employment and labour market participation, in transition countries the results indicate that more protection could contribute towards improving economic activity and employment performance.

10. All the labour market indicators analysed – labour market participation, employment, unemployment, youth unemployment and long-term unemployment – are positively affected by collective bargaining and active LMP. In addition, unemployment, and in particular long-term and youth unemployment, tend to rise with higher payroll taxes.

## 7.2 TWO MODELS OF LABOUR MANAGEMENT FOR THE TRANSITION COUNTRIES

Based on these findings and on our earlier analysis, two different models of labour management may be broadly distinguished in transition economies – one for the CSEE countries, including the Baltic States, and the other one for the CIS countries.

The CSEE countries have opted for a model that largely shifts responsibility for supporting redundant workers away from enterprises and onto public institutions, similar to practice in the EU countries. As described in this book, EPL has been greatly relaxed while national PES have been established, active LMP launched, unemployment insurance schemes introduced and social welfare programmes reshaped. Instead of maintaining labour hoarding, enterprises wishing to economize on labour costs dispose of excess workers either by directly laying them off with certain financial compensation fixed by law and collective agreement or push them to agree to leave voluntarily. In addition, enterprises have heavily reduced their human resource programmes and social services for workers. In the current situation of high unemployment, firms often prefer to recruit new workers with the desired work experience rather than invest in the retraining of their own staff or hiring school leavers with no work experience. Redundant workers then have the possibility of turning to the PES for re-employment assistance and income support, but whether they do so or not depends heavily on the access to and quality of employment services and LMP, as well as on the eligibility rules and the level of received income support, which vary greatly between countries. Similarly, the extent of workers' protection against lay-offs also varies between countries, as does the enforcement of national labour legislation.

The CIS countries, in contrast, continue to rely mainly on employment protection within enterprises, while assistance provided by PES is relatively poor. EPL tends to be rather restrictive, but employers themselves do not wish to escalate social tensions by firing under-used workers and rather opt for other forms of labour cost adjustment, such as short-term work, administrative leave or delayed wage payment while keeping workers on the payroll. Given the low demand for labour, coupled with the inferior quality of available vacant jobs, this solution appears more acceptable for all the parties. Employers can cut labour costs in line with their economic situation, save on severance pay and avoid destroying work-teams they will eventually need when market demand recovers; workers do not lose jobs that provide at least some income (which they often complement with income from other sources) and they maintain access to the social services still provided by their enterprise; and governments avoid the social unrest generated by unemployment and poverty.

In theory, the model for the CSEE countries facilitates better and faster adjustment flexibility for enterprises and stimulates more effective allocation of labour among sectors, with gains in terms of higher overall labour productivity. However, workers can benefit from the system only when the income support protects them well against any sharp fall in earnings and re-employment assistance is efficient enough to help them quickly find new jobs, otherwise it will lead to wider unemployment and lower participation rates. This is exactly the case of some CSEE countries, struggling with extremely high unemployment and inactivity levels that place a very high burden on their social welfare systems and still leave parts of their population in poverty.

In contrast, the model largely applied in the CIS tends to delay labour reallocation to new enterprises and trades offering more productive jobs, at the cost of lower labour productivity at the enterprise and the national level. While employment rates are in general higher and unemployment rates lower in this model, this does not mean that human capital is better utilized than in the first case or that this combination would lead to higher individual income levels. This would be the case if the enterprises were performing well and redeploying redundant workers to more productive jobs internally, but this is frequently not so. Instead, workers remain in their old, low-productivity jobs and supplement their incomes by work in second jobs of similarly low quality, resulting in a waste of human resources, while new high-quality jobs lack well-qualified applicants or may not be created at all because of a lack of workers with relevant skills.

## 7.3    CONCLUSIONS

Our analysis has clearly shown that the level of employment security perceived by workers is low and adversely affects their behaviour, with negative consequences for desirable labour mobility and flexibility. Policy conclusions and recommendations to address the causes of this perceived employment insecurity are outlined below.

There is now an urgent need in the transition countries to establish a new reasonable balance between adjustment flexibility for enterprises and employment and income security for workers, which would be acceptable to both sides and financially feasible and sustainable for public social funds. The approaching dates of the accession of ten transition countries from the CEECA to the EU make this goal even more imminent, as the national legislations and institutions have to comply with the European Social Charter.

To achieve this balance, the countries need first of all to review their national EPL and amend those provisions which ban necessary workforce adjustments for enterprises or make them too costly. Such provisions may force enterprises to turn to unlawful practices or cause discrimination against certain groups of workers. It has been proven by our comparative analysis that in many transition countries the overall EPL is reasonably liberal. Nevertheless, some rules may still be too restrictive, while others, especially those concerning irregular forms of employment, offer almost no protection to the workers concerned. The review and the subsequent legislative amendments should be achieved through social dialogue between the legislators and the social partners, but also with the involvement of associations representing less competitive groups of workers and jobseekers.

While this review of EPL is certainly important, it is also the case that in a number of transition countries the problem is not so much too strict or too liberal EPL but its weak enforcement in reality, such that workers' rights are left unprotected in the workplace. Employers make use of a poor labour market situation to threaten employees with dismissal and stigmatize them as "difficult" workers if they do not agree with conditions set by employers; the frightened workers then usually do not dare to complain. The level of unionization is relatively low at present, as in the majority of new small and medium-sized companies there are no trade unions to defend the legitimate rights of workers. Moreover, even if a union organization exists in the enterprise, workers themselves often do not trust it or are afraid of joining it because of threats from employers or enterprise managements. In many countries there are no dedicated labour courts, while civil courts may not always be attentive to claims brought by workers. In any case, these courts are overburdened, so it may take a long time to for a case to be heard. Even if the worker wins the case, he or she often has to leave the job in order to avoid future conflicts with the employer, so that apart from possible financial compensation the victory is often a Pyrrhic one, encouraging other employers in bad practices and discouraging workers from bringing complaints.

Higher payroll taxes lead to higher levels of aggregate, long-term and youth unemployment, according to our econometric analysis, but with the regression coefficients amounting to half of the value (and an opposite sign) of the coefficients of the active labour market policy variable for aggregate and long-term unemployment. Payroll taxes, by contrast, have no significant impact on employment and labour force participation rates. In general, unemployment schemes also seem to have no significant influence on labour market developments in the countries covered by our analysis. This finding, however, does not exclude the possibility of any other statistically significant effect in an individual country in certain periods of time as a consequence of changes in the two variables. Moreover, this conclusion has to be taken as tentative, as it may be affected by the form of indicators applied in our model. Therefore, in our further research we will endeavour to improve the specification of both variables to test their effects more precisely. Nevertheless, it is indisputable that if the transition countries wish to cut currently high unemployment rates and long-term unemployment, they need gradually to reduce extensive payroll taxes.

Conversely, collective bargaining and active LMP have been identified as having an important positive role to play in promoting employment and combating unemployment. This very important finding supports the ILO's position reflected in its Employment Policy Convention, 1964, No. 122, and also the EU employment policy guidelines to its Member States. These instruments advocate increased social dialogue in solving unemployment problems and in formulating and implementing employment promotion policy, and call for more intensive assistance to jobseekers in improving their employability and in job placement.

These conclusions regarding employment were also echoed in the High-level Tripartite Consultation on the Follow-up on the World Summit for Social Development for Selected Transition Economies, held in Budapest in January 1999 (see Nesporova, 1999). The policy recommendations adopted emphasized the need for stronger social dialogue extended to cover all-important economic and social issues affecting employment, unemployment and poverty, and complementing tripartite national negotiations by collective bargaining at branch, regional and enterprise levels. Moreover, the participants also agreed that tripartism would require not only the political will to engage in substantive dialogue, but also the full and equal engagement of independent, representative and competent social partners. Governments should support the enforcement of legislation ensuring the rights of workers to free collective bargaining and combat any open or hidden attempts of employers to ban or restrict trade unions in their enterprises. Also, trade unions should further gain workers' confidence by truly and consistently defending their rights and interests.

Similarly, the ILO's experience in the region points to the need to improve the extent and quality of employment services and active LMP such that they might reach a much wider range of jobseekers and provide appropriate but also cost-effective assistance for successful re-employment (see, again, Nesporova, 1999). In the first place, this requires further strengthening of the capacity and capability of the PES through increasing their staff resources (to achieve better ratios of PES staff to clients – jobseekers and employers), regular staff training, optimal decentralization of decision-making, improvement of premises and equipment of labour offices and better computerization of operations, development of sound networks and labour market databases, and better work organization. A lot more can be achieved through close partnerships of PES with governments at all levels, the enterprise sector, private employment agencies, education and training providers and non-governmental organizations.

At the same time, more emphasis should be placed on active labour market programmes to make them available to those jobseekers who can effectively gain from them in terms of improving their capacity and employability and finding a job more rapidly (optimally a regular one in the open market or subsidized employment that offers the opportunity to move eventually to regular employment). In line with the findings in Chapters 2 and 3, active labour market programmes should focus mainly on vulnerable and disadvantaged groups, to accommodate their needs, improve their skills and moderate their barriers to work. This concerns youths without work experience, workers with low or obsolete skills, people with disabilities, women or men with small children, older workers, ethnic minorities and ex-prisoners, many of whom cumulate several disadvantages and are jobless for extended periods of time, with a rapidly declining chance of return to employment. Active programmes should also be much extended in regions experiencing large-scale redundancies and high unemployment and underemployment, to contribute towards reducing regional labour market imbalances. In order to ensure the best interventions with a lasting effect, the programmes should be formulated after a thorough analysis of the causes of unemployment or forced inactivity, and the reasons why workers are not finding re-employment, and then combine appropriate measures addressing all these deficiencies.

Finally, it is important to remember that social dialogue and active LMP alone cannot solve unemployment problems in situations of substantial labour market imbalances and lack of demand for labour in the national or local markets. Recovery of demand for labour depends on the ability of the country or region to generate and sustain a high enough rate of economic growth, and to translate this into the creation of a sufficient number of new, good-quality jobs, replacing old, low-productivity jobs, while preserving existing good ones. The country's economic and social policies should actively stimulate economic growth and job creation by generating a favourable economic, legal and institutional environment for enterprises while making sure that the economic benefits are fairly shared by entrepreneurs and workers, and that workers enjoy reasonable employment and income security.

# BIBLIOGRAPHY

Akerlof, G. 1984. *An economic theorist's book of tales* (Cambridge, Cambridge University Press).

Arro, R.; Eamets, R.; Järve, J.; Kallaste, E.; Philips, K. 2001. *Labour market flexibility and employment security: Estonia*, Employment Paper Series, 2001/25 (Geneva, ILO).

Auer, P.; Cazes, S. 2000. "The resilience of the long-term employment relationship: Evidence from the industrialized countries", in *International Labour Review*, Vol. 39, No. 4, pp. 379–408.

Auer, P.; Cazes, S. (eds.). 2003. *Employment stability in an age of flexibility: Evidence from industrialized countries* (Geneva, ILO).

Bazen, S.; Martin, J.P. 1991. "The impact of the minimum wage on earnings and employment in France", in *OECD Economic Studies*, Vol. 16, spring, pp. 199–221.

Becker, G. 1964. *Human capital: A theoretical and empirical analysis, with special reference to education* (New York, Columbia University Press).

Beleva, I.; Tzanov, V. 2001. *Labour market flexibility and employment security: Bulgaria*, Employment Paper Series, 2001/30 (Geneva, ILO).

Bellmann, L.; Bender, S.; Hornsteiner, U. 2000. *Job tenure of two cohorts of young German men 1979–1990: An analysis of the (West-) German Employment Statistic Register Sample concerning multivariate failure times and unobserved heterogeneity*, IZA Discussion Paper No. 106 (Bonn, Institute for the Study of Labour).

Bertola, G. 1990. "Job security, employment and wages", in *European Economic Review*, Vol. 34, June, pp. 851–86.

Bertola, G.; Boeri, T.; Cazes, S. 1999. *Employment protection and labour market adjustment in OECD countries: Evolving institutions and variable enforcement*, Employment and Training Papers No. 48 (Geneva, ILO).

Bertola, G.; Boeri, T.; Cazes, S. 2000. "Employment protection in industrialized countries: The case for new indicators", in *International Labour Review*, Vol. 139, No. 1, pp. 57–72.

Blanchflower, D.; Oswald, A. 1994. *The wage curve* (Cambridge, MA, MIT Press).

Boeri, T. 1995. *Is job turnover countercyclical?* EUI Working Papers in Economics Series No. 12 (Florence, European University Institute).

Boeri, T. 2000. *Structural change, welfare systems, and labour reallocation: Lessons from the transition of formerly planned economies* (Oxford, Oxford University Press).

Bruno, C.; Cazes, S. 1998. *French youth unemployment: An overview*, ILO Employment and Training Papers No. 23 (Geneva, ILO).

Burgess, S.; Pacelli, L.; Rees, H. 1997. *Job tenure and labour market regulation: A comparison of Britain and Italy using micro data*, CEPR Discussion Paper No. 1712 (London, Centre for Economic Policy Research).

Burgess, S.; Rees, H. 1998. "A disaggregate analysis of the evolution of job tenure in Britain, 1975–1993", in *British Journal of Industrial Relations*, Vol. 36, No. 4, Dec., pp. 629–55.

Calmfors, L; Driffill, J. 1988. "Bargaining structure, corporatism and macroeconomic performance", in *Economic Policy*, No. 6, pp. 13-61.

Casale, G. (ed.). 1999. *Social dialogue in Central and Eastern Europe* (Budapest, ILO Central and Eastern European Team).

Cazes, S.; Nesporova, A. 2001. *Towards a new trade-off between labour market flexibility and employment security for the transition countries*, Employment Paper Series 2001/23 (Geneva, ILO).

Clarke, S. 1998. *Making ends meet in a non-monetary market economy*, mimeo, Centre for Comparative Labour Studies, University of Warwick, available at www.warwick.ac.uk/russia/endsmeet.doc.

Cornia, G.A.; Paniccià, R. (eds.). 2000. *The mortality crisis in transitional economies* (Oxford, Oxford University Press).

Emerson, M. 1988. "Regulation or deregulation of the labour market: Policy regimes for the recruitment and dismissal of employees in the industrialized countries", in *European Economic Review*, No. 32, No. 4, pp. 775–817.

Esping-Andersen, G. 1990. *The three worlds of welfare capitalism* (Princeton, Princeton University Press).

——. 2000. "Who is harmed by labour market regulations?", in G. Esping-Andersen and M. Regini (eds.): *Why deregulate markets?* (Oxford, Oxford University Press).

European Bank for Reconstruction and Development (EBRD). 2000. *Transition Report 2000: Employment, skills and transition* (London).

European Commission (EC). 2001. *Employment in Europe 2000* (Brussels).

Eurostat, 2001. *Employment and labour market in Central European countries*, Nos. 2 and 3 (Luxembourg).

Faggio, G.; Konings, J. 2000. *Job creation, job destruction and employment growth in transition countries in the '90s*, IZA Discussion Paper No. 242 (Bonn, Institute for the Study of Labour).

Gimpelson, V.; Lippoldt, D. 1997. "Labour turnover in the Russian economy", in OECD: *Labour market dynamics in the Russian Federation* (Paris), pp. 17–57.

Haltiwanger, J.; Vodopivec, M. 1998. *Gross worker and job flow in a transition economy: An analysis of Estonia*, mimeo, University of Maryland, MD.

Hartog, J. 1999. *The Netherlands: So what's so special about the Dutch model?* Employment and Training Papers No. 54 (Geneva, ILO).

Ichniowski, C.; Shaw, K.; Prennushi, G. 1997. *The effects of human resource management practices on productivity*, NBER Working Paper No. 5333 (Cambridge, MA, National Bureau of Economic Research).

International Labour Organization (ILO). 1996. *World Employment 1996/97: National policies in a global context* (Geneva).

——. 1997. *World Labour Report, 1997–98* (Geneva).

——. 1999. *Decent work*, Report of the Director-General, International Labour Conference, 87th Session (Geneva).

——. 2000. *Organization, bargaining and dialogue for development in a globalizing world*, GB.279/WP/SDG/2, paper presented to the 279th Session of the ILO Governing Body, November (Geneva).

——. 2002. *Global Employment Agenda: Discussion paper*, March (Geneva).

ISSA Database, www.issa.org.

Komarek, V. et al. 1990. *Prognoza a program* [Prognosis and programme] (Prague, Academia).

Kostrubiec, S. 1999. *Unregistered employment in Poland in 1998* (Warsaw, Central Statistical Office).

Kwiatkowski, E.; Socha, M.; Sztanderska, U. 2001. *Labour market flexibility, employment and social security: Poland*, Employment Paper Series 2001/28 (Geneva, ILO).

Layard, R.; Nickell, S.; Jackman, R. 1991. *Unemployment: Macroeconomic performance and the labour market* (Oxford, Oxford University Press).

Lehmann, H.; Wadsworth, J. 2000. *Tenures that shook the world: Worker turnover in Russia, Poland and Britain*, CEP Discussion Papers No. 459 (London, London School of Economics and Political Science).

Lindbeck, A.; Snower, D. 2001. "Insiders versus outsiders", in *Journal of Economic Perspectives*, Vol. 15, No.1, pp. 165–88.

Mincer, J. 1976. "Unemployment effects of minimum wages", in *Journal of Political Economy*, Vol. 84, No. 4, August, pp. S87–104.

Ministry of Labour and Social Development of the Russian Federation. 1998. *Employment Programme 1998–2000* (Moscow).

Nesporova, A. 1993. "Measuring employment in Central and Eastern Europe", in OECD: *Employment and unemployment in economies in transition: Conceptual and measurement issues* (Paris).

——. 1999. *Employment and labour market policies in transition economies* (Geneva, ILO).

Nickell, S. 1987. "Why is wage inflation so high?", in *Oxford Bulletin of Economics and Statistics*, Vol. 49, No. 1, pp. 103–28.

——. 1997. "Unemployment and labour market rigidities: Europe versus North America", in *Journal of Economic Perspectives*, Vol. 11, No. 3, pp. 55–74.

——; Layard, R. 1999. "Labour market institutions and economic performance", in O. Ashenfelter and D. Card (eds.): *Handbook of labour economics*, Vol. 3 (Amsterdam and New York, Elsevier), pp. 3029–84.

O'Leary, C.; Nesporova, A.; Samodorov, A. 2001. *Manual on evaluation of labour market policies in transition economies* (Geneva, ILO).

Organisation for Economic Co-operation and Development (OECD). 1994a. *Jobs Study*.

——. 1994b. *Employment Outlook 1994*.

——. 1996. *Employment Outlook 1996*.

——. 1997. *Employment Outlook 1997*.

——. 1999. *Employment Outlook 1999*.

——. 2001. *Employment Outlook 2001*.

Piore, M. 1986. *Labor market flexibility* (Berkeley, CA, University of California Press).

Pissarides, C. 2001. "Employment protection", in *Labour Economics*, Vol. 8, No. 2, pp. 131–59.

Riboud, M.; Silva-Jauregui, C.; Sanchez-Paramo, C. 2002. "Does Eurosclerosis matter? Institutional reform and labor market performance in Central and Eastern European countries", in B. Funck and L. Pizzati (eds.): *Labor, employment, and social policies in the EU enlargement process* (Washington, DC, World Bank).

Scarpetta, S. 1996. "Assessing the role of labour market policies and institutional settings on unemployment: A cross-country study", in *OECD Economic Studies No. 26*, pp. 43–98.

Simagin, Y. 1998. "Ob otsenkakh masshtabov dopolnitel'noy zanyatosti naseleniya" [On estimates of the size of additional (secondary) employment of the population], in *Voprosy ekonomiki*, No. 1, pp. 99–104.

Sorm, V.; Terrell, K. 1999. *A comparative look at labour mobility in the Czech Republic: Where have all the workers gone?* CEPR Discussion Paper No. 2263, Transition Economics Series (London, Centre for Economic Policy Research).

Tchetvernina, T. 1998. "Russian unemployment in the mid-1990s: Features and problems", in S. Clarke (ed.): *Structural adjustment without mass unemployment?* (Cheltenham, Edward Elgar), pp. 256–75.

——. 1999. *Russian labour market: Trends, institutions, policy*, background paper prepared for the ILO (Geneva, ILO).

——. ; Moskovskaya, A.; Soboleva, I.; Stepantchikova, N. 2001. *Labour market flexibility, employment and social security: Russian Federation*, Employment Papers Series 2001/31 (Geneva, ILO).

Traxler, F.; Kittel, B. 1997. "The bargaining structure, its context and performance", paper presented at the conference on Economic Internationalization and Democracy, University of Vienna, Dec. 14–15.

United Nations Children's Fund (UNICEF). 2001. *A decade of transition*, Regional Monitoring Report No. 8 (Florence, UNICEF Innocenti Research Centre).

United Nations Economic Commission for Europe (UNECE). 1998. *Economic Survey of Europe*, No. 3 (Geneva).

——. 2000. *Economic Survey of Europe*, Nos. 1 and 2 (Geneva).

——. 2001. *Economic Survey of Europe*, No. 2 (Geneva).

Varshavskaya, L.; Donova, I. 1998. *Vtorichnaya zanyatost' naseleniya* [Secondary employment of the population], mimeo, Centre for Comparative Labour Studies, University of Warwick, available at www.warwick.ac.uk/russia/secemp.exe.

Večerník, J. 2001. *Labour market flexibility and employment security: Czech Republic*, Employment Papers Series 2001/27 (Geneva, ILO).

Visser, J. 1990. "In search of inclusive unionism", in *Bulletin of Comparative Labour Relations*, Vol. 18, pp. 1–278.

Williamson, J. 1990. "What Washington means by policy reform", in J. Williamson (ed.): *Latin American adjustment: How much has happened?* (Washington, DC, Institute for International Economics).

Williamson, O.E. 1985. *Economic institutions of capitalism: Firms, markets, relational contracting* (New York, Free Press).

World Bank. 2001. *Poland – Labour market study. The challenge of job creation* (Washington, DC).

# INDEX

Note: Bold page numbers refer to tables and figures; footnotes are shown as subscript numbers.